P9-DDC-529

CAROLYNE ROEHM

# *Winter* NOTEBOOK

**CAROLYNE ROEHM**

**WINTER NOTEBOOK**



HarperCollins books may be purchased for
educational, business, or sales promotional use.
For further information please write
Special Markets Department
HarperCollins Publishers, Inc.
10 East 53rd Street
New York, NY 10022

FIRST EDITION

ISBN 0-06-019452-9
99 00 01 02 03 ❖/HK 10 9 8 7 6 5 4 3 2 1

CAROLYNE ROEHM

# *Winter* NOTEBOOK

*Garden Hearth Traditions Home*

PHOTOGRAPHY BY
SYLVIE BECQUET ALAN RICHARDSON

DESIGN BY DINA DELL'ARCIPRETE-HOUSER WRITTEN WITH MELISSA DAVIS

HarperCollins*Publishers*

The Garden Book

*welcome to the*

# NOTEBOOK

Winter is the most encouraging season for the gardener. It is the only time of the year when the creative juices of the plantsman are given free reign. The frozen ground may not give way to a shovel, but it does yield to the fertile imagination. Spurred by stacks of plant and seed catalogues and garden books, I pick up colored pencils and graph paper to plot the spring plantings. This year, I promise myself, the beds and borders will be spectacular, the weather will work with me and the pests will be defeated. There are no earthly obstacles in January; I am a fount of optimism. By mid-July I will find that some of my hopes were misplaced. The too-pink poppies will look frightening next to the veronica, or the squash beetles may have done a number on the curcurbits. But during the dormant season my glass is half full. My completed vellum plans are a precise rendering of beds in elegant hues, neatly boxed and defined. For a few cold months my gardens are perfect, at least on paper. Seduced by promises of better hybrids and heirlooms my seed orders in February become bigger every year. By mid-March, every available shelf in the greenhouse and hoophouses brims with hope: scores of flats of eager seedlings that will surpass whatever variety they replaced last year. The 25 varieties of seed potatoes I ordered in a fit of spud madness arrive, and I remember that the peas will need sowing before the spring solstice. A daring planting of early lettuces, mâche and spinach struggle the coldframe surrounded by a late March snow. The hellebores have followed the snowdrops and push up their buds before St. Patrick's Day. In winter, I am surrounded by potential. My house weatherstone burned to the ground this winter. But it, too, like an eager perennial pushing through the snow, will rise again and be more beautiful than before.

page 114
page 54
page 62
page 16
page 76
page 84
page 100
page 120
page 2
CHRISTMAS DINNER
DECEMBER 24, 1999
PURÉE OF CHESTNUT SOUP
COQ AU VIN WITH WILD MUSHROOMS
HERBED ORZO
PURÉE OF LEEKS, FENNEL AND PEAS
ENDIVE WITH STILTON AND APPLES
WARM GINGERBREAD
WITH WHIPPED CREAM AND CARAMEL SAUCE
CHASSAGNE-MONTRACHET 1995
page 44

# CONTENTS

## *Winter*

# HELLEBORES

When I first started gardening, I was drawn to dramatic colors and forms: the cobalt blue of delphinium, the startling crimson of a tissue paper poppy or the sensual assault of an unfolding double peony. I eventually learned that this razzmatazz was not altogether approved of by the horticultural elite. The understated hellebore was much more to their liking. Gertrude Jekyll's writings dictated harmony of foliage and color in the border. Subtlety, not showbiz, was her mantra. • The older I became, the more I appreciated the refinement of many things in life, including the hellebore. True, it is one of the only blossoms to make a winter appearance, but the hellebore has other merits. Their muted coloring is infinitely more sophisticated and adaptable than my flashier loves. Now that I have built my own woodland patch of hellebores, I am more adventurous with their mauve, cream, yellow, peach, purple, wine, crimson and blue-gray blossoms. I bring them into the house and pair them with just one or two other flower varieties, or as a leading player in a mixed bouquet. • Other late-winter bloomers such as aconites, snowdrops and crocuses can claim their charms, without demanding very much of me. To experience the self-possessed finesse of the hellebore, however, you have to see them closely. Hellebores do not hold their heads up to us, so we must go to them. I crouch into the thawing soil and inspect them at ground level, lifting their flowers up with a forefinger. When I see the purple-black sepals surrounding a collar of chartreuse nectaries and the center dotted all over with jolly ivory anthers, I know that spring can't be too far off.

## GROWING HELLEBORES

Unlike other perennials, hellebores cannot be easily or frequently divided. Older plants may be divided, but they are slow to reestablish themselves, and it can be two years before the new divisions flower. *Helleborus orientalis* hybrids, with their more defined root system, are easier to divide than the species hellebores with their confusing mass of rizomes. Hellebores also cannot be reproduced by stem or root cuttings, hence the high costs of nursery-grown plants. Keep in mind that when buying named varieties of plants, purchase plants in flower to be sure of coloration.

Since *Helleborus orientalis* is such a prolific self-seeder, the simplest way to increase your stock is to let the plants drop their seed in the fall and germinate. The color of the offsprings' flowers, although varied and sometimes interesting, will not be a perfect replica of the parent plant, and over time the self-sown blossoms will become muddy. Since it may be three years before a seed-sown plant blooms, however, it is wiser to buy seed from a breeder. Hellebores are easy to hand cross, but ripe seed pods must be protected in cotton bags or the pods will burst and scatter the seed.

Start seed as soon as it arrives or is collected. Plant the fresh seeds in a commercial seed-starting mix at least an inch apart and cover with ½ inch of moist sand. Cover pot with plastic wrap to keep humidity high; germination can take anywhere from 50 to 550 days, according to Thompson & Morgan, so be patient. (Neither light nor cold-treatment is necessary for germination). Once a set of true leaves have formed, prick out the plants and either repot, place in a nursery bed, or plant the seedlings where they are to grow in the garden.

Most hellebores are easily started from seed, and prefer light shade and humusy soil. They are hardy from Zones 5 to 9 with the exception of *Helleborus niger* which is hardy to Zone 3. *Opposite:* Hybrids of *Helleborus orientalis* show great variation in color, spotting, streaking and blossum size. Although many vegetatively propogated (cloned) varieties are named, growers usually sell "strains" of hybrid *orientalis*. A strain is grown from seed and will be similar to the parent in bloom size and color, but it will not be identical.

**TIP**

*If drooping flower heads are a problem with your hellebore cultivar, cut the stems to half an inch and float the buds barely touching face up in a bowl of cool water.*

HELLEBORES' MUTED SHADES NATURALLY FLATTER MY FAVORITE COLOR COMBINATION OF MAUVES AND GREENS

Freckled hellebores, snowball viburnum and coral ranunculus are paired with nodding green spikes of *Helleborus argutifolius* (*detail left*).

# holiday hellebore

*Helleborus niger,* more commonly called the Christmas rose, blooms in its native environment (the mountains of central Europe) in mid-winter, weeks before the Lenten rose, *Helleborus orientalis.* Legend links the hardy perennial with the birth of Christ and a shepherdess named Madelon. As Madelon tended her sheep one winter night, wise men and other shepherds passed by the snow-covered field where she stood, offering gifts for the newborn Christ Child. As she saw the wise men's rich gifts of gold, frankincense and myrrh. Madelon began to weep at the thought of having nothing, not even a simple flower for Jesus. An angel, seeing her tears, brushed away the snow revealing a most beautiful white flower tipped with pink, the Christmas rose. After hearing this sweet story, I found that the poinsettia couldn't compete with such a beautiful provenance.

*Clockwise from top left:* During Christmas I gave *Helleborus orientalis* in a roughly thrown pot; a specimen of *Helleborus niger* in terra cotta rimed with moss; and a spike of *Helleborus argutifolius* (the Corsican hellebore), as hostess gifts. I plucked a single white bloom of the Christmas rose and tucked it under the ribbon a few minutes before this present was offered.

Limonium latifolium (Sea Lavender)
Hoya carnosa (Wax)
Calosia argentea (Purple Flamingo)
Fritillaria meleagris (Snake's Head Lily)
Helleborus orientalis (unnamed hybrid hellebore)
Helleborus orientalis (unnamed hybrid hellebore)
Prunus cerasifera 'Nigra' (Cherry Plum)

CHECKERED FRITILLARIA AND SPECKLED HELLEBORES SHOW TEXTURES AND PATTERNS AT PLAY

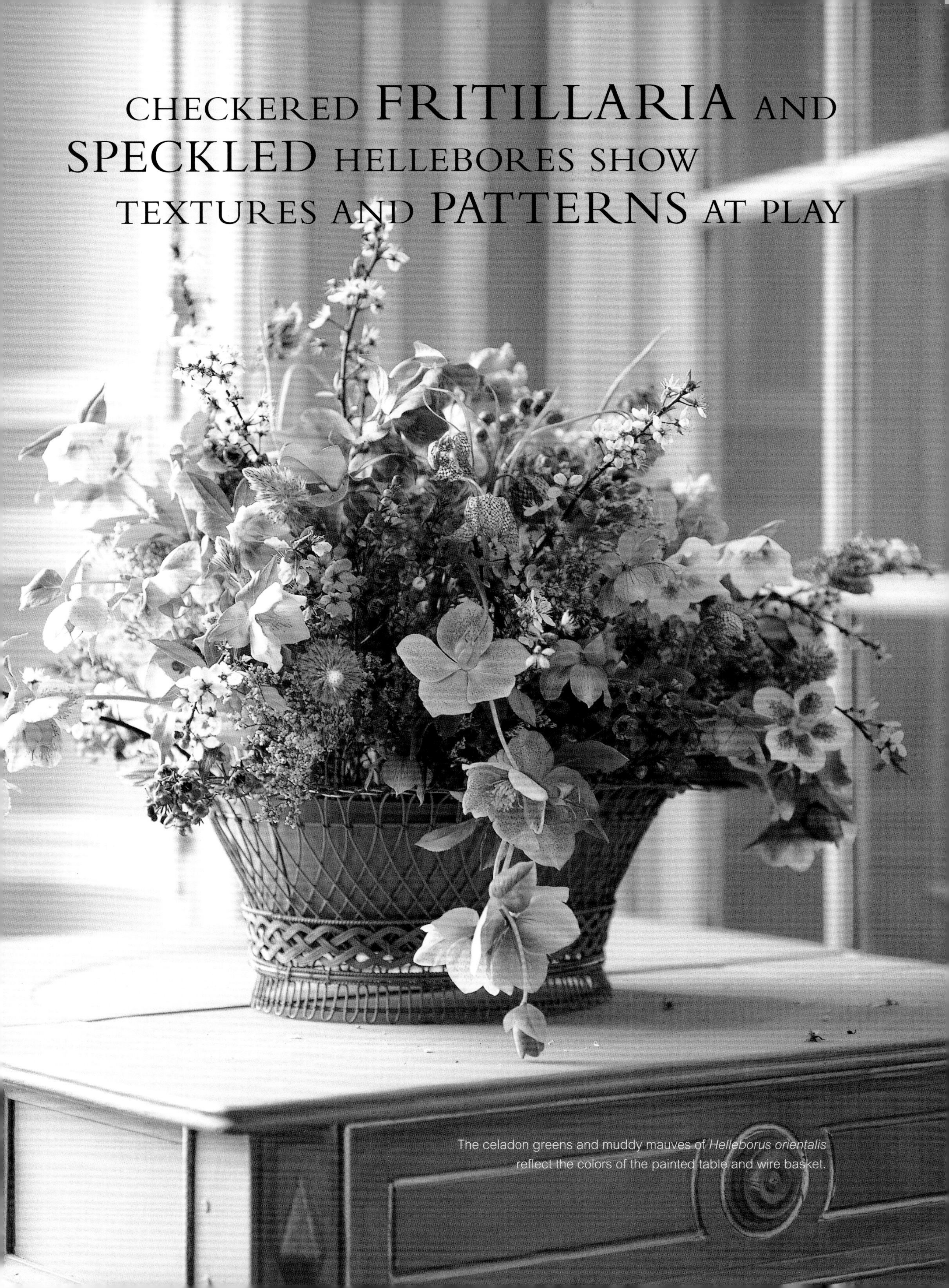

The celadon greens and muddy mauves of *Helleborus orientalis* reflect the colors of the painted table and wire basket.

*Left:* Before the guests arrived, I clipped a single hellebore flower to decorate the crystal service plates. Once the plates were removed, each place was set with a green foil-wrapped gift bound in green ribbon (*bottom*).

*Above center and left:* Motivated by the hellebores' palette of purple and green, I set my dinner table with clear olive Venetian goblets and green glass plates that absorbed the green walls of the room. Using that as a base, I built the flower arrangement with peony tulips in mid purple, adding viburnum, checkered *Fritillaria meleagris* and lacy *Limonium latifolium* in a rusted urn. Variegated ivy was woven through the candelabra, which helped flow the arrangement into the tabletop. The green and white linens covering the table anchored the setting.

## HELLEBORE FAVORITES

Most often named varities are sold as "strains," meaning they are not identical to the mother plant, but close in flower size and color.

### SPECIES

*H. argutifolius*

*H. niger*

### PURPLE TO BLACK

*H. orientalis* 'Garnet'

*H. orientalis* 'Queen of the Night'

*H. orientalis* 'Tom Wilson'

### PINK

*H. niger* Blackthorn Strain

*H. orientalis* 'Dawn'

*H. orientalis* Ballard Strain

### WHITE

*H. niger* 'Potter's Wheel'

### YELLOW

*H. orientalis* 'Blowsy'

### GREEN

*H. orientalis* 'Celedon'

*H. orientalis* 'Green Cups'

*H. orientalis* x *H. virdis* 'Old Ugly'

### SPOTTED

*H. orientalis* 'Philip Wilson'

spotted McLewin Strain

ADDITIONAL NOTES / INSPIRATIONS / REMEMBER NEXT YEAR

decorating
entertaining

gift wrapping
gift giving

# HOLIDAY PLANNING

*The more human beings proceed by plan, the more effectively they may hit by accident.*
*—Friedrich Dürenmatt*

I remember with horror the Christmas eves of years past when I was practically in tears because I had attempted to buy too much, create too much and go too much. I was so exhausted by my own disorganization that I missed the whole fa-la-la point. I have now pared down my holiday festivities to more realistic expectations, and I am much more organized. In fact, the better prepared I am for a party, a speech or a holiday celebration, the less frazzled I am when the inevitable disruption of my plans comes. Last-minute dinner guest cancellations, gifts ordered weeks in advance that never arrive, the snowstorm that hits the day of the party and feuding relatives who won't sit next to each other are just a few of the aggravations that have to be dealt with at this stressful time of year. But I find that if I just ride out the bumps and relax, armed with a mightly to-do list and notated calendar, I have much more fun and fewer hassles. I review my notes each year before the holiday onslaught, and find that they help me make quicker work of decorating, gift wrapping, entertaining and gift giving. One thing I have found since keeping notes and photos in my journal is that I no longer feel I have to reinvent the wheel and come up with a new decorating scheme every Christmas. Recycled menus and decorations are perfectly acceptable. After all, isn't that how traditions are born?

I have been collecting antique and new glass ornaments (*opposite*) from around the world for decades. Friends have also given me ornaments (terriers being a favorite subject). I forget about the ornaments in the months they have been in tissue-paper storage, but Christmas brings a renewed delight as I hang them on the tree. Each one triggers a thought or an old memory that reminds me where I was at that time in my life, and there is a story for each. With only lights and ornaments to decorate its branches, the trimmed tree is transformed into a scrapbook. I should call it my memento tree.

*From top left:* A wreath made from freeze-dried fruits, berries and greens will last from season to season. The topiary studded with limes is built on a base of chicken wire pierced with boxwood clippings, as are the topiaries in the wicker baskets (*bottom left*). We used a ready-made wreath and garland from the florist then added rhododendron leaves, eucalyptus berries and unripe coffee beans.

Shake-
speare
Shake-
speare
QUEEN
ANNE

For a small Christmas dinner in my New York apartment, I was anxious to move outside the restraint of traditional red and green, but I didn't want to go so far afield that the decorations didn't say "Noel." As I usually do when looking for inspiration, I opened an art book and was immediately taken by the chiaroscuro reds of a Zurbaran painting. The deep red in the painting reminded me of a swatch of antique fabric with gold threads I had collected. I put the two color clues together and came up with the idea for the antique gold wreath, gold foil-wrapped packages and ribbon. The backdrop of red leather and gold embossed books was a perfect showcase for the bouquet of 'Black Magic' and 'Mercedes' roses collared with gold-painted galax leaves.

## HOW TO MAKE THE WREATH

***What you will need:***

- 2 14-inch wire frame hoops
- Spool of 22-gauge wire
- 3 bunches lemon leaves
- 2 pounds boxwood
- 2 pounds holly
- 3 cans gold floral spray paint
- 14 6-inch floral picks
- 14 limes
- Floral foam (optional)

***How-to:***

Wire the hoops together (for added strength). Pick through lemon leaf bunches and separate from main branch. Each sprig should have 3 to 4 leaves and be approximately 7 inches long. Sort through boxwood and separate into sprigs as with lemon leaves. Repeat with holly. Lay all sprigs on newspaper and spray with gold paint (*top left*). Pierce limes at stem end with floral picks and push half way through limes. Stand limes in floral foam or set in glasses to prepare for spraying. Spray limes with gold paint and let dry. Make bunches (*top right*): gather 4 or 5 stems of lemon leaves, 2 of boxwood and 2 of holly, mixing sprig types in bundles. Going counterclockwise, lay bunched sprigs on hoop (with stem ends toward you). Wire stem ends to hoop (*bottom left*). Repeat with bunches, overlapping and hiding previous stem ends with next bunch. When placing the last bunch to complete the circle, cut the stems shorter, about 2 or 3 inches, to hide the hole where the circle meets. Wire final bunch onto hoop. Pierce limes at an angle into wreath (*bottom right*) where wired stem ends of bunches meet hoop (for stability). Touch up with spray paint if necessary. Attach wire loop in back of wreath and hang.

## TIP

*When making leaf bunches, stagger layers while facing leaves forward and keeping in mind that the bunches should be more flat than domed, like a nosegay bundle.*

# decorating journal

## POINTS TO REMEMBER

- *If you are using fresh decorations, think "accessibility." Use greens from your backyard, which can be replenished when they start to dry.*
- *Keep it simple, go for volume rather than variety. An oversized bouquet of holly is more effective than the same size arrangement of fussy mixed greens.*
- *Splurge on a detail such as a few yards of silk ribbon or a beautiful gift card.*
- *For long-lasting garlands, build them in a base of floral foam set on a tray (ready-made trays hold two 9-inch blocks of foam) and water daily.*
- *If time is short, make a pyramid of red glass Christmas balls glued together as your centerpiece.*
- *For a tidy geometric table decoration, line up small pots of miniature poinsettias down the center of the dinner table and surround them with a rectangle of evergreens or holly.*
- *Use packing straw instead of moss to blanket and hide the potting soil in live arrangements.*

THEMES: ______________________________

EXTERIOR: ______________________________

INTERIOR: ______________________________

SUPPLIES / SOURCES:

ADDITIONAL NOTES / INSPIRATIONS:

COMMENTS / RESULTS:

REMEMBER NEXT YEAR:

# gift giving

Since shopping and making presents are two of my favorite winter activities, I find that it is better to give than receive. During this season of intensive entertaining, host and hostess presents must be in constant production. If I am shopping for a present, I try to stay away from the pragmatic and veer towards the fanciful. I keep my gifts simple if homemade–cookies, fruit pyramids, potted plants, and small flower arrangements–but present them in fine containers or elegantly decorated boxes. I address the gifts with a special stamp-on oak tag (*opposite*) or have a shipping tag made up at the local printer.

*Clockwise from top left:* It may look good enough to eat, but the open-mesh basket lined with moss and topped with clementines and kumquats is only for show—the fruit has been glued to stay put. A gingerbread house (not of my own making) is always an appreciated present. Christmas offerings can be as simple as a small silver cup of carnations, or fresh herbs planted in attractive crocks nestled in a basket.

ROEHM

## NANCY'S SPICED SUGAR COOKIES

*Makes about 3 dozen*

3 cups flour
1½ cups butter
1½ cups brown sugar
1 teaspoon salt
2 (or more) tablespoons milk
3 teaspoons cinnamon
1 teaspoon ground cloves
1 teaspoon ground nutmeg

**1.** Preheat oven to 350° F. Put all ingredients together in a large bowl. Knead with fingers until all ingredients are well mixed. Add more milk if necessary to form into a ball. Chill.
**2.** Roll out dough to about ⅛ inch thick. Cut with cookie cutters and place on greased cookie sheet. Bake for 8 to 10 minutes or until browned.

## Royal Icing

*Makes 3 cups*

3 tablespoons meringue powder
4 cups confectioners' sugar
5 to 6 tablespoons warm water
Food coloring (optional)

Beat together all ingredients with an electric mixer until icing forms peaks, about 10 minutes. If stiffer icing is needed add one tablespoon less water.

## MITTIE ANN'S SUGARED PECANS

*Makes 1 pound*

1 pound pecan halves
1 egg white
1 teaspoon cold water
1 cup sugar
1 teaspoon cinnamon
1 teaspoon salt

**1.** Preheat oven to 250° F. Beat egg white with water until fluffy.
**2.** Fold pecans into egg whites until well coated.
**3.** Mix cinnamon, sugar and salt. Fold coated pecans into sugar mix. Bake on a cookie sheet for 1 hour. Serve.

*Left:* A sphagnum moss bear holds a sliver beaker of scented jasmine vine. Two plastic pots of maidenhair fern from the supermarket were repotted in twin wicker baskets. *Below:* Mini poinsettias, also from the supermarket, were repotted into small silver-plate beakers and topped with moss. *Below right:* Two simple gifts, a pineapple in a nest of boxwood and a vine covered heart, with personalized tags.

## TIP

*Presentation is everything. Common plants, or fruits, in plastic pots from the grocery store can be transformed into charming gifts if repotted into baskets or porcelain pots and footed with moss, grass or boxwood clippings.*

# *gift-giving journal*

## POINTS TO REMEMBER

- *Using your address book as a guide, write a master list of the names of all gift recipients. From this list you can begin a gift journal noting gift ideas, gifts given, gifts received and thank-you notes to write.*
- *Divide gift obligations into categories such as close friends, family, neighbors and business contacts. Don't forget service people (mail carrier, sanitation workers, doormen, fire fighters, etc.).*
- *Stock up on packing and shipping supplies if you are not sending gifts via mail order.*
- *Make a separate list for catalogue gifts. Keep notes on order number, customer service number or invoice number. If possible, order all catalogue items on the same day for easier record keeping.*
- *If you are giving baked goods, stock up on parchment paper, tissue paper, tins, bags and bakery boxes.*

MAIL ORDER (BUSINESS): ______________________________

______________________________

______________________________

______________________________

MAIL ORDER (PERSONAL): ______________________________

______________________________

______________________________

______________________________

HOMEMADE GIFTS: ______________________________

______________________________

______________________________

______________________________

DONATIONS:

GRATUITIES:

ADDITIONAL NOTES / COMMENTS:

REMEMBER NEXT YEAR:

# gift wrapping

When it comes to gift wrap, I am a pack rat. I never throw anything away. I also scout paper and craft stores year round for interesting wrappings. I keep all my squirreled gems in large plastic storage boxes: one for ribbons, one for cards and tags and one for attachments such as leaves and berries (*opposite*). When holiday time comes around, I pull out my boxes, take snipped samples from each and arrange them into color groups. With the small samples laid before me, I find it easier to match up ribbons and cards with wrapping paper and to experiment with new color combinations.

*Clockwise from top left:* Separating paper, ribbons and tags into color groups of muddied browns and greens, carmine reds, greens and blues together and strict blues helps make quick work of wrapping chores. By taking small cuttings and samples of my collected supplies, I find it easier to mix and match color combinations, which means I am less likely to make a mistake when I finally wrap the gifts.

Although I sometimes go overboard with imported ribbons and handmade papers when wrapping special gifts, most of my wrappings are inexpensive and simple. The ivy wrapping *(above)* comes from a floral supply company (florists use it to wrap bouquets), the name tags are plant identification sticks and the ribbon comes from a discount material store. Tags can also be made from old Christmas cards by cutting off the front of the card with scalloped-edged or wavy-edged shears and writing a message on the back. Even the deluxe packages *(opposite)* topped with gold poppy heads, frosted lemons, faux apples and glass berries can be deceiving: the white package *(top right)* is wrapped in freezer paper and the fruit toppings were taken off an old wreath.

## TIP

*If expensive papers are out of the question, cheat a little. Use freezer wrap or butcher paper (splurge on the ribbon) and decorate the paper with a rubber stamp and gold ink. Galax leaves, ivy or dried poppy heads sprayed gold make attractive attachments. Save silk and velvet ribbons and refresh with an iron before reusing. Use a hole punch (never tape!) to attach cards to ribbon ends.*

**HOW TO WRAP A BOX** Pleat two sheets of tissue paper to fit dimensions of box. Center one tissue north-south, another east-west, and push down into box, leaving tissue hanging over edge. Put gift in box. Fold tissue paper edges over gift. With top on box, turn box upside down and place in center of gift wrap. Measure paper against box (trimming sides of paper about 3/4 the depth of box) and cut. Fold paper half way around box and tape. Fold under other raw edge about 1/2 inch. Affix double-sided tape to folded edge. Fold corners *(as shown)* and affix with double-sided tape. Repeat corner folds on other end of box.

**HOW TO TIE A BOW** Wrap ribbon around box *(as shown)*. Tie a knot and cut ribbon leaving 6-inch tails. Using two colors of ribbon, form a loop with the ribbon (use half the width of the box to estimate size of loop). Continue to form loops, pinching in the middle, until four loops are formed on each side (you may have more loops if you are using only one strand of ribbon). Still holding pinched center, position bow on box knot, and tie bow onto package with ribbon tails. Pull to separate bow and plump loops. Punch hole in corner of gift card and thread onto ribbon tail.

# *gift-wrapping journal*

## POINTS TO REMEMBER

- *Think beyond the traditional color group of red and green for holiday gift wrappings; try light green and rich deep brown, or a monochromatic scheme.*
- *Collect tags, ribbons, ornaments, baskets, beakers, pots, etc., throughout the year and stash them away. When the holidays arrive, you won't be faced with last-minute panic and store leftovers.*
- *Check floral supply stores, art stores and superstore craft sections for package additions for the tops of gifts.*
- *If you don't have time to wrap each gift, stock up on inexpensive containers such as take-out containers, bakery boxes or paper bags that can be tied with gift cord or raffia.*
- *Collect dried flowers such as Queen Anne's Lace or poppy heads and spray paint gold for gift toppings. Also, save hemlock cones and glue into star clusters for gift toppings.*
- *Save good ribbons and refresh with an iron before reusing.*
- *Save elegant Christmas cards and recycle as gift tags or holiday recipe cards.*

THEMES: ______________________________

______________________________

______________________________

COLOR COMBINATIONS: ______________________________

______________________________

______________________________

WRAPPING ACCESSORIES: ______________________________

______________________________

______________________________

______________________________

SUPPLIES / SOURCES:

ADDITIONAL NOTES / INSPIRATIONS:

COMMENTS / RESULTS:

REMEMBER NEXT YEAR:

We usually think of the holiday season as a time for entertaining hoards of guests and relatives. But sometimes it is nice to bring tidings of comfort and joy to just one special person. I arranged this dinner to exchange gifts with such a person, but kept the theme very low key, plain red and white, and very small. Individual bouquets of white hellebores and roses, and roses alone, were clustered in gold cups small enough to peer over during dinner. As luck would have it, a favorite damask tablecloth (*opposite*) turned out to have the same red tones as the roses and ribbons. The only light in the room came from candles, casting a golden warmth. It was the perfect setting for an intimate exchange of gifts.

*Clockwise from top left:* For this romantic holiday dinner for two, I made each place setting small and personal with individual nosegays of roses and violets in gold beakers. Plain white wrapping paper was paired with a wide deep red ribbon topped with sprayed lemon leaves and a single hellebore that matched the hellebore and rose bouquet. Tiny champagne buckets hold a wee glass wine flask.

*Above and right:* If I am in a hurry to pull a holiday table together for impromptu gatherings, I try to lift a theme I've used before and adapt it to a new situation. The burlap table cloth was borrowed from a Halloween barn dinner dance. I substituted trailing ivy for bittersweet vines and made a centerpiece of a cypress tree surrounded by mini cypress trees in wicker baskets. Wicker baskets also held candy olives and Christmas cookies.

## HOW TO MAKE THE CARNATION TREE

***What you will need:***

3 blocks (3-by-4-by-9 inches) floral foam
Pedestal container (6 inches diameter)
6 18-inch floral sticks
6 to 7 dozen red carnations (depending on bloom size)

***How-to:***

Soak foam in hot water according to package instructions. Stand the first two blocks of floral foam on end in the container. Trim corners of foam to make a cone shape (*top right*). Trim edges and corners off third block of foam, leaving top flat, and secure to foam base with six floral sticks (*middle right*), piercing the foam at an angle. Break sticks when necessary if too long.

Working from the bottom up, pierce foam at an angle (*bottom right*) with carnations. Carnation stems at the bottom of the tree should be 4 to 5 inches long. As you progress up the tree, stems will need to be cut shorter.

## TIP

*To keep the tree throughout the holidays, remove it to a cool place at night. Check daily for water. When watering, place tree in the sink and slowly pour warm water over top of tree and allow it to soak to the bottom. (The top of the tree will dry out faster than the bottom.)*

# *entertaining journal*

## POINTS TO REMEMBER

- *Entertain only if you want to and you truly enjoy it. Don't allow your annual party to become a rote because you have Christmas burnout. A small gathering can be more thoughtful...and manageable.*
- *If you are having a sizable gathering, keep the menu and the decorations simple. Stick to a few elements—too many visual bits and pieces are confusing.*
- *Don't depend on a menu that calls for perfect timing. Use chaffing dishes to keep foods warm. Buffet-style foods are best.*
- *'Tis the season to make lists. Buy a notebook (with pockets for receipts) to designate as your holiday entertaining journal. You can look at lists from years past to jog your memory for holiday tasks and entertaining ideas.*
- *Iron napkins with scented linen water, an old Provençal tradition now coming back into fashion.*

THEMES: ______________________________

______________________________

______________________________

______________________________

______________________________

MUSIC: ______________________________

______________________________

______________________________

______________________________

CATERER: ______________________________

______________________________

______________________________

PARTY RENTALS: ______________________________

______________________________

______________________________

SUPPLIES / SOURCES: ______________________________

______________________________

______________________________

______________________________

ADDITIONAL NOTES / INSPIRATIONS: ______________________________

______________________________

______________________________

______________________________

______________________________

COMMENTS / RESULTS: ______________________________

______________________________

______________________________

______________________________

REMEMBER NEXT YEAR: ______________________________

______________________________

______________________________

______________________________

# A CHRISTMAS PARTY

When I see the candles glowing, the silver and red balls glistening, the crystal gleaming; when I smell the fragrance of balsam in the air and hear the laughter of good friends and family, all the stress of planning and preparation for the holidays disappears. It is the end I must keep in mind, not grappling with the means. I think, to a man, that we find the holidays the most angst-ridden time of year. Too much to do, too little time. This year, I pared my celebrations down to one event: a dinner party in my cottage, jokingly referred to as "Weatherpebble." The cottage is dominated by one large rustic room, formerly a home for carriages, that accommodated two 14-foot Christmas trees. These firs were my single extravagance. I raided the discount stores for tree decorations–white fairy lights, red glass balls and red florist ribbon—to lay on thick. Because of the scale of the trees, the simple scheme was very effective. I made tablecloths from red felt, scalloping the edges with pinking shears, and laid them over a felt drop of olive green. A splashy display of color, I thought, for only $1.99 a yard. I bought 50 cranberry red wine glasses at $2.99 each, not because I had invited 50 people, but because they looked so dazzling lined up together. Who says Christmas decorations have to be orthodox? After a fabulous dinner (thank you, Nancy) we were entertained by nine glorious voices singing peace on earth, good will to men. And for that moment, there was. Merry Christmas.

## PARTY POINTS TO KEEP IN MIND

Organization is the panacea for holiday stress, although something stronger is sometimes called for. But before I can even think about raising my glass to the near and dear, I have to actually find the glasses. Here are some tips taken from my to-do list that may help you keep your party planning friction-free:

• Select your party dates early, this is a heavily booked time of year. Sniff out your close friends for other parties that might conflict. Write up a guest list (with backups) and call to confirm that the date is free, then send the invitations. Record RSVPs. Two days before the party, confirm the final list.

• While waiting for RSVPs, select a theme such as ice-skating or caroling. If your theme is dependent on the weather, have a back-up theme that isn't.

• Find and engage entertainment. This can be as simple as bribing the local 6th-grade class with cookies in exchange for carols, or shelling out for a professional group. School music teachers or church choir members often know of off-beat groups such as Elizabethan madrigal singers or Gregorian chanters.

• If it's a big bash, order party rental supplies, estimate what you will need (tables, chairs, glasses, flatware, linens, serving trays, candles, food warmer, etc.), and order a month ahead. When the guest list is set, call the rental company with your revised order.

• Select the menu to reflect the formality or casualness of your party. Seated or buffet? This is not the time to experiment with new dishes. Go with the tried and true and tested.

• Prices for florist greens and flowers rise this time of year. Scout the countryside for free evergreen snippings. Clip greens a week before the party, spray with water daily, and keep in a cool garage until ready to assemble the day before the party.

• Order specialty foods such as Smithfield hams or stone crabs early, especially if you are buying via mail order. Order wines and spirits.

### *Menu*

*Gravlax with Mustard Dill Sauce*
*Mittie Ann's Sugared Pecans*
*Purée of Chestnut Soup*
*Coq au Vin*
*Herbed Orzo*
*Purée of Leeks, Fennel and Peas*
*Endive with Stilton and Apples*
*Warm Gingerbread with Whipped Cream and Caramel Sauce*

*personal notes:*

**Favorite Christmas Music**

*Emmylou Harris:*
*"Light of the Stable"*
*Frank Sinatra:*
*"A Jolly Christmas from Frank Sinatra"*
*Harry Connick, Jr.:*
*"When My Heart Finds Christmas"*
*Aaron Neville:*
*"Aaron Neville's Soulful Christmas"*
*Boys Choir of Harlem:*
*"Christmas Carols and Sacred Songs"*
*Nat King Cole:*
*"The Christmas Song"*
*Ella Fitzgerald:*
*"Ella Fitzgerald's Christmas"*

Cranberry wineglasses (*left*) were decorative as well as useful. After I have called the guests, I sent the invitation (*below left*), then called again to confirm the guest list. *Below right:* I used red florist ribbon to make a large bow, then draped the tails of the ribbon down the trees.

## TIP

*Left: As a safety precaution, use candlestick wax to secure the candles. If the candle is too large for the holder, set the stem of the candle in a half inch of hot tap water to soften the wax on the outside of the candle. Push the candle into the holder gently. Repeat if necessary.*

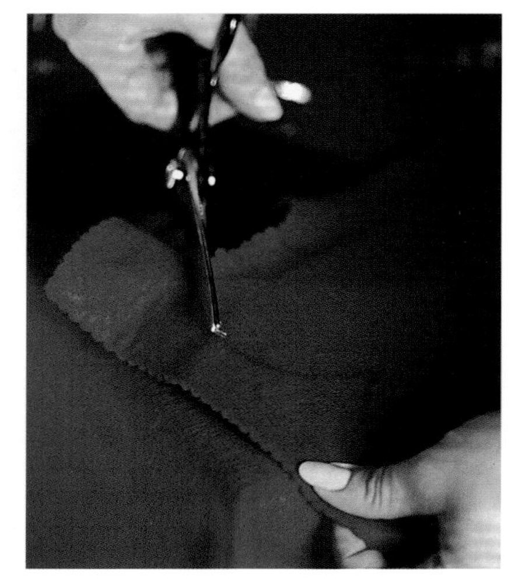

*Top:* Food preparation begins the day before the party. We make sure all the ingredients are in place. The day of the party, we iron the napkins, lay the tablecloths, set the table and begin the seating chart. *Middle:* The felt table is scalloped with pinking shears. Margarita designates a place for coats and boots. *Bottom:* Nancy begins assembling the table decorations. Chairs have been rented and are ready to be put at the table. Placido checks the tables and gives the crystal a quick buff to make sure that everything is gleaming.

A FEW FINISHING TOUCHES SHARPEN UP THE TABLE. ALL IS GLEAMING AND THE PARTY CAN BEGIN

*Above:* At the last minute, we figure out the seating and put the place cards on each napkin. The holiday CDs are selected and stacked in the player for background music. The fireplaces and candles are lighted and their soft glow warm the room. Miniature evergreens in silver-plated pots and old-fashioned red mercury balls in silver cups add an additional sparkle. *Right:* My friend and neighbor, Charlie Irish, lends a hand and helps pour the wine.

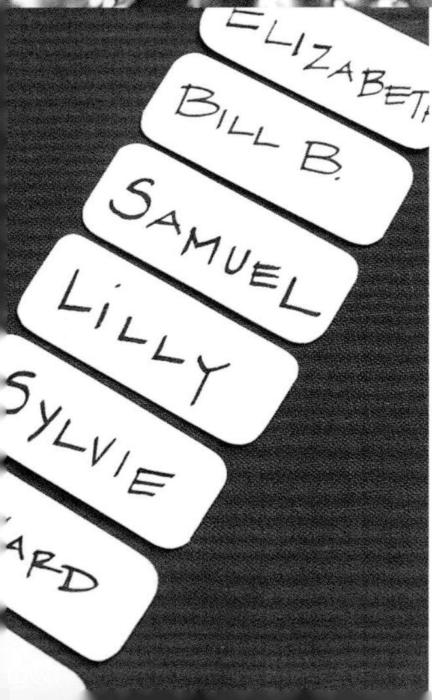

The guests are finally seated and a happy hum of conversation begins. As I look back over the room where friends and family have gathered, I realize that all the preparations for the party have been worth it.

We found a fabulous group of singers—though they had never actually sung together before—and they amazed us all with their spirit and talent. After they performed carols and religious songs, my mother (*above*) who has always been a tough musical critic, applauded the loudest.

idaho
red new
all blue
yellow new
russet
fingerling
yukon gold

# POTATOES

A steaming baked potato, slathered in butter and topped with a too-generous dollop of sour cream, is my reward food. If I've been uncharacteristically good (stayed on diet, practiced piano regularly, read boring but edifying book, denied self purchase) I don't turn to chocolate or truffles or caviar, but to that mother of all comfort foods. If suddenly all foods were taken from me, it is the humble potato I would miss the most. I usually grow a few plants in the vegetable garden, but not enough to slake my cravings. My growing space is limited. This year Nora, my head gardener, discovered potato bins. The seven black plastic bins were something of an eyesore so they were set up away from the formal potager, next to the chicken coop. The bins were filled with two dozen different varieties of potato seed layered in compost and straw. French fingerlings, purple Peruvians, shocking pinks, buttery yellows, waxy reds, creamy whites and netted russets grew in the same amount of space that, without the bins, would have accommodated about six plants. Our yields were amazingly prolific, and instead of having to dig up the compacted soil to find the tubers, we just lifted the bins, brushed away the straw and out tumbled a rainbow of unblemished potatoes. We now have enough potatoes in our make-shift root cellar for a winter's worth of spud lust. To house our potatoes we dug a hole in the potager, built a little hut out of straw bales around the hole, laid in our supply of potatoes and put more straw on top to keep them warm. If we don't eat all the tubers before the really cold weather comes, we shall see if our root cellar experiment works.

## WINTER'S END SHEPHERD'S PIE

*Serves 6 to 8*

- 2 tablespoons melted butter
- 2 tablespoons olive oil
- 1½ to 2 pounds ground sirloin
- 2 medium onions, chopped
- 4 cloves garlic, minced
- 3 tablespoons tomato paste
- 2 cups beef broth or water
- ½ tablespoon dried oregano
- ½ tablespoon dried basil
- ¼ cup chopped fresh parsley
- Salt and freshly ground pepper
- 2 cups fresh or frozen corn kernels
- 6 cups mashed potatoes (see Colcannon recipe, but omit sour cream and add ¼ cup olive oil)

**1.** Preheat oven to 375°. Grease a large 13 × 9 inch casserole (or 6 large individual souffle dishes) with 1 tablespoon of the butter. In a large heavy skillet, heat ½ tablespoon olive oil. Crumble half of the beef into the very hot pan and cook over high heat until browned, 3 to 5 minutes. Transfer to a bowl with a slotted spoon and repeat with the remaining beef.

**2.** Add the remaining olive oil to the drippings in the skillet and lower heat to medium. Add onions and garlic and sauté until transparent, about 5 minutes. Return the beef and any meat juices to the skillet and stir in the tomato paste.

**3.** Stir in beef broth, oregano, basil and parsley and simmer 10 minutes. Add salt and pepper to taste.

**4.** If making individual servings, divide beef mixture among souffle dishes and top with ⅓ cup corn kernels, and 1 cup mashed potatoes; otherwise add beef mixture to casserole, add corn, and top with a layer of mashed potatoes. Brush surface with remaining melted butter and bake for 30 minutes or until potatoes are golden.

## RÖSTI (SWISS POTATO PANCAKES)

*Serves 6*

- 7 medium russet potatoes, peeled
- 4 shallots, grated
- 3 tablespoons chopped parsley
- 1 teaspoon salt
- 1 teaspoon freshly ground pepper
- Olive oil
- 1 cup creme fraiche or sour cream
- 2 to 3 tablespoons chopped chives

**1.** Preheat oven to 300°. Grate potatoes in a food processor or with a hand grater. In 2 batches, transfer the potatoes to a kitchen towel and wring out as much water as possible.

**2.** Transfer potatoes to a large bowl, add grated shallots, parsley, salt and pepper; toss well.

**3.** In a 7-inch omelet pan, heat ½ tablespoon of olive oil. Add ½ cup of grated potatoes and flatten to fill the pan.

**4.** Cook each side for 4 minutes, or until golden brown and crisp. Repeat with remaining potatoes. Transfer each rösti to a large rack set on a baking sheet. Reheat in the oven to crisp up, about 6 minutes. Top with creme fraiche or sour cream and chives. Serve immediately.

## POTATOES DAUPHINOISE

*Serves 6 to 8*

2 tablespoons olive oil
5 cloves garlic, minced
4 anchovy filets
2 cups whole milk
1 cup chicken stock
1 cup heavy cream
1 tablespoon butter
7 russet potatoes, peeled and thinly sliced
1 large onion, thinly sliced
2 cups shredded Gruyere

**1.** Preheat oven to 350°. In a medium saucepan, stir olive oil, garlic and anchovies and cook over medium heat until anchovies are melted, about 3 minutes.
**2.** Add milk, chicken stock and heavy cream; bring to a boil. Reduce heat and simmer for 5 minutes.
**3.** Generously butter a large, 13 × 9 inch casserole. In the casserole, spread half of the potatoes in an overlapping layer. Spread half of the onions on the potatoes and add half of the shredded cheese. Repeat layers, ending with cheese.
**4.** Pour milk mixture on top of potatoes. Bake until potatoes are tender and top is golden, about 45 minutes. Let sit for 15 to 20 minutes before serving.

## SPICY BRAISED POTATOES WITH CIPPOLINI ONIONS

*Serves 6*

¼ cup olive oil
1½ pounds cippolini onions, peeled
5 to 6 cloves garlic, finely chopped
1 medium chili pepper, finely chopped
8 medium purple potatoes*, washed and quartered
Salt and freshly ground pepper
1 cup dry white wine
1 cup chicken stock
Juice of ½ lemon
¼ teaspoon powdered saffron
½ cup chopped parsley

**1.** In a large (12-inch) skillet, heat olive oil. Add onions and sauté over medium heat until golden but not cooked through, about 8 minutes.
**2.** Add garlic, chili pepper and potatoes and cook, stirring, another 4 to 5 minutes. Season with salt and pepper.
**3.** Add white wine and, stirring occasionally, boil to reduce for 5 minutes. Add chicken stock, lemon juice and saffron, and stir well. Cover and simmer 15 to 20 minutes until potatoes are tender.
**4.** Add parsley and cook uncovered until sauce is thick and syrupy, 1 to 2 minutes.

*Purple potatoes will turn slightly grayish when cooked. However, this does not affect their flavor.

## MARGARIDA'S FRITTATA

*Serves 6*

4 russet potatoes, peeled and diced
3 tablespoons olive oil
2 cloves garlic
Salt and freshly ground black pepper to taste
½ cup each coarsely chopped red peppers, orange peppers, baby portobello mushrooms, onions
½ cup peas
½ cup chopped parsley
8 large eggs
Salt and freshly ground pepper to taste

**1.** Preheat oven to 350°. In a large pot of boiling salted water, parboil the potatoes about 8 minutes. The potatoes should still be firm. Drain in a colander.

**2.** In a large cast iron skillet, heat the olive oil. Add garlic and sauté over moderate heat until golden. Remove garlic. Add the chopped vegetables to the skillet and sauté until translucent, about 8 minutes. Add potatoes and continue to cook for another 3 minutes. Add peas and parsley and sauté for 2 minutes.

**3.** Beat eggs with salt and pepper. Pour beaten eggs over vegetable mixture. Remove from stove.

**4.** Put skillet in upper third of the oven and cook until eggs are set, about15 minutes. Serve immediately.

## WARM WINTER POTATO SALAD

*Serves 6*

2½ pounds fingerling potatoes, washed and patted dry
2 tablespoons olive oil
3 to 4 sprigs fresh rosemary or 2 tablespoons dried
½ teaspoon freshly ground pepper
5 to 6 ounces Stilton cheese, crumbled

**1.** Preheat oven to 375°. Cut fingerlings into 1-inch pieces and spread on a large baking sheet. Coat potatoes with olive oil and rosemary. Roast potatoes, tossing occasionally until tender, about 25 minutes.

**2.** Remove from oven and toss immediately with Stilton and pepper until cheese is slightly melted. Serve immediately.

*The recipe Gateau Buerre, pictured above, is adapted from* A Passion for Potatoes *by Lydie Marshall.*

## GATEAU BEURRE

*Makes one 11-inch round loaf*

**1¼ pounds russet potatoes, unpeeled**
**½ cup milk**
**2 teaspoon active dry yeast**
**2 teaspoons sugar**
**4 cups or more all-purpose flour**
**1 tablespoon salt**
**6 tablespoons butter**
**Salt and freshly ground pepper**

1. Cover unpeeled potatoes with cold salted water and bring to a boil. Partially cover and cook for 30 minutes or until tender.
2. Preheat oven to 300°. Drain potatoes, reserving ½ cup potato water. Add milk to potato water. Sprinkle yeast and sugar over potato water and set aside in a warm place for 15 minutes.
3. Dry potatoes in oven for 10 minutes. Peel potatoes and mash, one potato at a time. Set aside to cool.
4. Add salt to flour and mix. Put yeast mixture in a large bowl. With a wooden spoon, gradually beat in the mashed potatoes and then add the flour ¼ cup at a time at first then tablespoon by tablespoon. When the dough gets too stiff, knead with your hands until all 4 cups are incorporated. Knead in more flour if the dough is very sticky. Continue to knead until dough is smooth.
5. Preheat oven to 425°. Let dough rest in a large bowl covered with plastic wrap until it has doubled in size. Sprinkle flour on the dough and knead for about 1 minute, adding more flour. The dough should be very soft.
6. Butter an 11-inch pan with a removable bottom. Flour your hands and spread the dough in the pan. Scatter the butter all over the top, then sprinkle with salt and pepper.
7. Bake on a cookie sheet in the middle of the oven for 10 minutes, or until the top is lightly golden brown. Cut into wedges and serve.

## COLCANNON

*Serves 6 to 8*

**8 russet potatoes, peeled and quartered**
**1 cup sour cream**
**1 cup hot milk**
**4 tablespoons butter**
**Salt and freshly ground pepper**
**1 small head cabbage, chopped**
**2 medium onions, chopped**
**4 cloves garlic, minced**

1. In a large saucepan, cook potatoes in boiling water until tender; about 25 minutes. Drain and mash with a hand masher. Add sour cream, milk and half of the butter and mash well. Add salt and pepper to taste.
2. Meanwhile, in a medium saucepan of boiling water, cook the cabbage until almost tender, about 5 minutes; drain in a colander.
3. In a large skillet, melt the remaining butter and sauté onions and garlic over medium heat until transparent, about 5 minutes. Add cabbage and cook another 5 minutes or until tender. Season with salt and pepper.
4. Fold cabbage mixture into mashed potatoes and serve immediately.

# WEATHERSTONE POTATO CHART

| VARIETY | USES | TASTE | MATURITY | COLOR |
|---|---|---|---|---|
| All Blue | Mash | Mealy | Late | Deep blue skin, blue flesh |
| All Red | Boil, steam | Waxy | Mid-season | Red skin, pink flesh |
| Bintje | All-purpose | Waxy with some starch | Late | Gold skin, yellow flesh |
| Butte | Bake | High protein, high vitamin C, less mealy | Late | Russet skin, white flesh |
| Caribe | Mash | Smooth, satiny | Early | Lavender skin, white flesh |
| Carola | Bake, steam | Rich taste, waxy | Late | Medium yellow skin, yellow flesh |
| Cherry Red | Boil, steam | Slightly waxy, moist, new potato | Early | Red skin, white flesh |
| Desirée | All-purpose | Moist, creamy | Late | Rosy skin, white flesh |
| Gold Nugget | Bake, boil, steam | Buttery | Mid-season | Russet type, yellow flesh |
| Green Mountain | Mash | Moist, mealy | Late | Half Russet skin, white flesh |
| Irish Cobbler | Excellent mashed | Mealy | Early | White skin, white flesh |
| Katahdin | All-purpose | Good flavor | Mid-season | Thin white skin, white flesh |
| Kennebec | All-purpose standard | smooth texture | Mid-season | White skin, white flesh |
| Krantz | Bake | mash | Early | Russet type, white flesh |
| Ozette | Boil, steam, salads | Earthy, flaky, creamy | Late | Fingerling, thin yellow skin, yellow flesh |
| Red Dale | Bake, boil, steam | Sweet, some starch | Early | Red skin, white flesh |
| Red Norland | New potato | Waxy, good flavor | Very early | Thin red skin, white flesh |
| Red Pontiac | Boil, steam, new potato | Waxy, moister than Norland | Mid-season | Thin red skin, crisp white flesh |
| Rose Finn Apple | Boil, steam, salads | Excellent flavor, waxy, firm | Late | Fingerling, rosy skin, yellow flesh |
| Russet Burbank | Bake | Flaky, mealy | Mid-season | Russet skin, white flesh |
| Russian Banana | All-purpose, best for salads | Firm flesh | Late | Fingerling, yellow flesh |
| Shepody | French fries, baked | Mealy, dry | Early | White skin, white flesh |
| Viking Purple | All-purpose, microwave | Creamy, moist light | Early | Purple skin, pure white flesh |
| Yellow Finn | Bake, boil, fried | Mealy, starchier than Yukon Gold | Late | Yellow skin, yellow flesh |
| Yukon Gold | Bake, boil, steam | Very buttery | Early | Yellow skin, yellow flesh |

**BAKING POTATO:** Russets or Idahos with thick netted skins. Mealy textured flesh suitable for baking, mashing or frying.
**WHITE POTATO:** Thin skins, finer textured flesh than baking potatoes. All-purpose uses.
**YELLOW POTATO:** Thin skins with waxy but buttery flesh suitable for boiling, steaming, roasting or frying.
**RED POTATO:** Thin red skins, waxy, crisp flesh. Suitable for boiling, steaming, roasting.
**NEW POTATO:** Any immature potato. Tender, sweet flesh. Suitable for boiling, steaming, roasting.
**FINGERLING POTATO:** Small, oblong, prolific, and firm. Great for roasting and salads.

ADDITIONAL NOTES / INSPIRATIONS / REMEMBER NEXT YEAR

# CARNATIONS

Carnations usually do not solicit kind reactions, even from people who have few opinions about flowers. Naysayers dislike their smell or shape or easy availability—all assets in my mind—or their dowdy overuse. Like the equally slandered marigold (another picked-on favorite of mine), carnations suffer abuse from misuse, not from any inherent ugliness. There is much to commend about them. Unlike many hybridized florist flowers, carnations actually do give off a scent, a clean but exotic clove-like aroma. The finely cut saw-toothed edges of the petals introduce unusual texture, shadow and depth when paired with more uniform petals. The fact that they are sold everywhere all winter long, from corner convenience stores to supermarkets, means that at a moment's notice you can grab a few dozen to lighten up a room depressed by gray winter days. Best of all, carnations are inexpensive—less than half the cost of roses—and long-lasting. A properly conditioned arrangement of carnations will last 10 to 12 days, enough to make it through the holidays. • Blame the floral delivery business for corrupting the perpetual-flowering dianthus, as they are technically called, but erase from your mind the image of dyed carnations paired with sterile ferns and a sad spray of baby's breath. Instead, picture deep-red carnations paired with velvety carmine roses, or snowy carnations teamed with white stock, variegated holly and eucalyptus berries. Even a simple bundle of three dozen same-color carnations displayed in a cut-crystal bowl can elegantly dominate a winter table; no other additions are necessary to make the bouquet the center of attention. To show them at their best, gather the flowers so the heads are displayed in a tight dome. Carnations need to be closely nestled to their neighbor, the parts taken as a whole, to avoid prom-night tackiness. Carnations are quick to please. Give them another chance.

A mix of French florist carnations, punctuated by a single white bloom, are gathered into a nosegay and displayed in a blue and white pedestal vase.

BOLD PINK FRENCH CARNATIONS GROUPED IN CELADON VASES MAKE A QUICK, CLEVER STATEMENT

by themselves

I had just gotten off the plane in Paris when a friend called and asked to drop by for a drink. Not wanting my visitor to feel unwelcome, I quickly ran to the corner florist and grabbed three dozen bold pink carnations tipped in paler pink. Within fifteen minutes, I had the flowers grouped in five inexpensive celadon pots on the mantle, the white wine was on ice, and my hair was combed. When my guest arrived, he immediately noticed the clove scent of the flowers and commented on their beauty. My minimal, low-labor effort immediately set the mood for a lovely relaxed chat.

*Far left:* Bright hot pink carnations with sharply serrated edges show well even when loosely structured. *Left and middle left:* Don't be afraid to use rich colors that may seem, at first glance, to clash. I borrowed the risky pairing of magenta and red from the 1950s fashion designer Elsa Schiaparelli, whose signature color was hot pink. *Opposite page:* Tints of pink, coral and creamy yellow come together in a gold porcelain beaker. To make the arrangement a bit less formal, I have used unopened and partially opened buds (*also middle right*) to loosen up the domed structure of the bouquet.

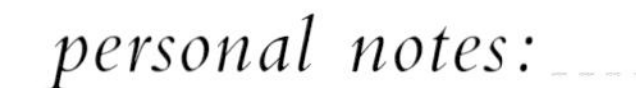

*personal notes:*

## HOW TO MAKE THE BOUQUET

***Tools Needed:***

Scissors
Floral tape
Round bowl, about 10 inches in diameter
Plastic liner (optional)

***Flowers used:***

60 (approximately) galax leaves
7 dozen (approximately) peppermint carnations

***How-to:***

The number of nosegays needed depends on the size of the container used (I used a 10-inch Paul Revere silver bowl fitted with a plastic liner). The instructions should be adapted to the size of your flowers and container.

Gather 7 to 9 carnations (depending on bloom size) into a bundle forming a nosegay, and cut stems to about 6 inches. Crown carnation bundle with about 5 galax leaves, serrated edges pointing outward. Working from the top of the nosegay, bind bundled stems with overlapping florist tape. Set finished nosegay aside in warm water. Repeat making nosegays until you have enough to fit snuggly in your container. You will need about 10 nosegays for a 10-inch bowl. Arrange the nosegays in a lined container filled with fresh warm water, snipping stems as needed (the stems of the middle nosegays will be longer than those on the perimeter) fit your container.

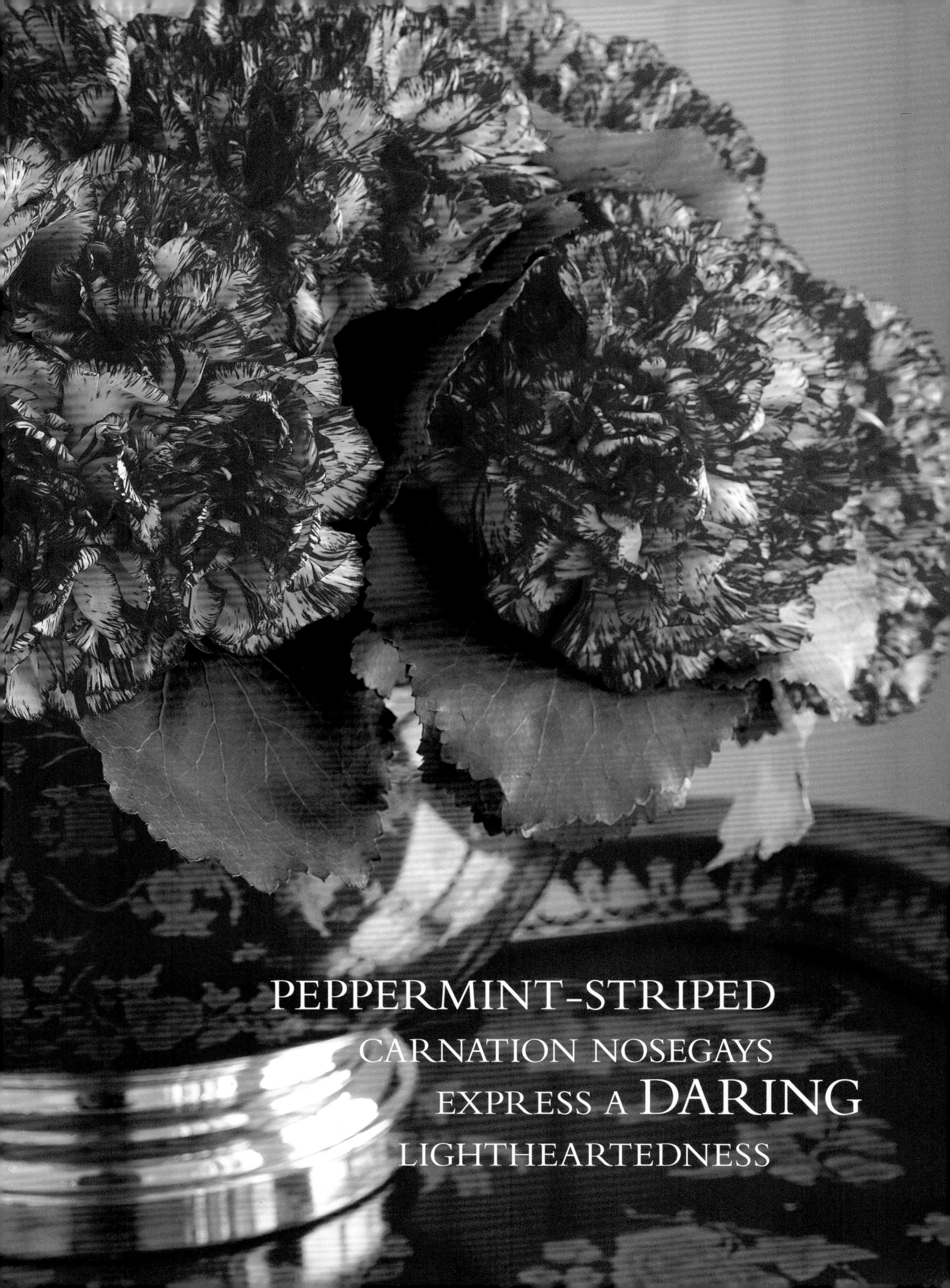

PEPPERMINT-STRIPED
CARNATION NOSEGAYS
EXPRESS A DARING
LIGHTHEARTEDNESS

Euonymus 'Aureomarginatus' surrounds a beaker of red carnations and blue hyacinths.

# mixing it up

One of the many virtues of the carnation is its ability to introduce an almost giddy texture to formal bouquets. The fine saw-tooth picotee edges lessen the gravity of serious red roses (*above*) and lighten the rigidity of the column-shaped hybrid hyacinths (*opposite*). A more practical plus is the carnation's ability to pad out big expensive rose bouquets that would otherwise consume your entire floral budget. The ambitious bouquet (*above*) in a 20-inch silver soup tureen required about 12 dozen roses. Had it not been for the adaptable carnations, the arrangement would have needed an exorbitant 24 dozen roses.

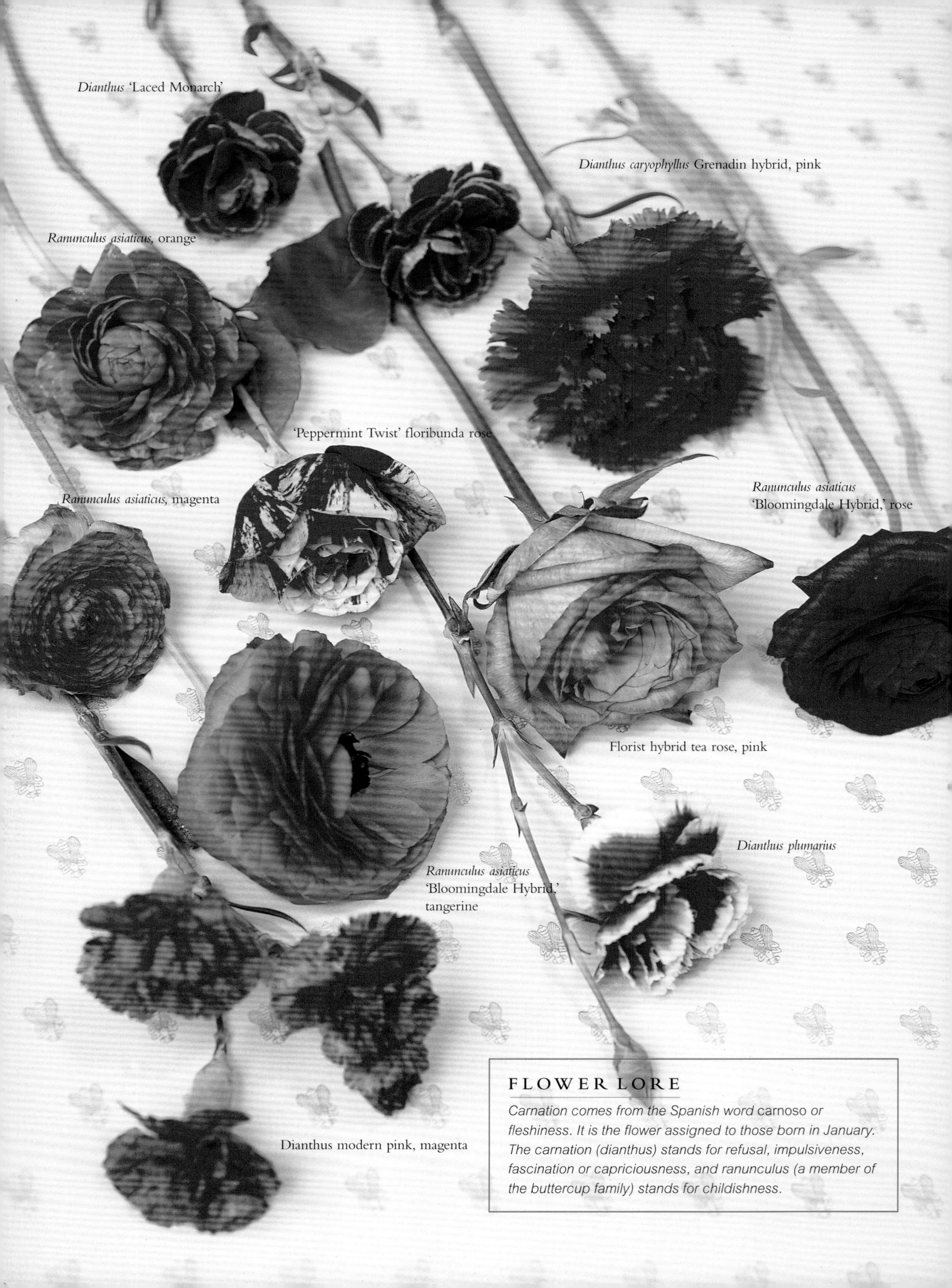

*Dianthus* 'Laced Monarch'

*Dianthus caryophyllus* Grenadin hybrid, pink

*Ranunculus asiaticus*, orange

'Peppermint Twist' floribunda rose

*Ranunculus asiaticus*, magenta

*Ranunculus asiaticus*
'Bloomingdale Hybrid,' rose

Florist hybrid tea rose, pink

*Dianthus plumarius*

*Ranunculus asiaticus*
'Bloomingdale Hybrid,'
tangerine

Dianthus modern pink, magenta

## FLOWER LORE

*Carnation comes from the Spanish word* carnoso *or fleshiness. It is the flower assigned to those born in January. The carnation (dianthus) stands for refusal, impulsiveness, fascination or capriciousness, and ranunculus (a member of the buttercup family) stands for childishness.*

# ELECTRIC PINK AND ORANGE WHORLED BUDS ERASE THE GLOOM OF WINTER

Roses, carnations and ranunculus, *(identified left)*, fill a black marble pedestal vase.

*Left:* Daffodils share a crystal vase with striped carnations. *Below:* Pink ranunculus and *Dianthus caryophyllus* bring out the blues of bachelor buttons and hyacinth.

*Above:* Nosegays of miniature roses highlight peachy pink carnations in a brass cache pot. *Right:* Streaked and swirled carnations team up with daffodils in a simple porcelain pot. *Opposite:* Chartreuse chrysanthemums and *Hydrangea arborescens* stream through deep red carnations while Granny Smith apples play out the theme.

# MILLENNIUM GOOD LUCK LUNCH

I've heard so much media yammering about the coming millennium that by the time those zeros roll around, I'm going to feel quite underwhelmed. In an effort to outdo each other, many people are planning intricate parties and celebrations. I'll admit, I did feel the pressure to compete, but after some deliberation it became clear to me that the best way to celebrate would be to stay home–especially if the world was going to end–and have an intimate gathering with the usual kith and kin. Knowing that I would not be able to stage a spectacle that would meet the expectations of the last eve of the century, I decided to have a low-key New Year's Day lunch. When mulling over a theme for my table, I elected to defy the gloomy prognosticators and instead try to promote feelings of good luck and new beginnings. I opted for a miniature orange tree instead of cut flowers in the center of the table to evoke life and growth. According to legend, round objects denote prosperity, so I will set a bowl of kumquats at each place. Also, each guest will be given a gift to give them luck in the coming year. As for my New Years Eve plans? Sorry. Can't make it. I have to stay home and prepare for the arrival of my guests. I intend to toast the new century with a vintage bottle of champagne in front of a roaring fire, surrounded by a few loved ones.

Black-eyed peas are a Southern staple thanks to excellent PR from George Washington Carver, but the legumes are particularly unavoidable on New Year's day. The custom of serving the peas on the first day of the year stems from the belief that they will bring good luck to whoever eats them. There are countless recipes for cooking the beans, but the most popular is called "Hoppin' John." One theory on the origin of the dish's name is that the children of the family were asked to hop around the table once before sitting down to eat, and another says the name was merely an invitation for guests to "hop in and join" the meal. My recipe for black-eyed peas is an adaption of the traditional one, that Nancy, the Weatherstone chef created. Nancy's Black-Eyed Peas will be featured at my Millennium lunch, followed by a clever four-leaf-clover-covered horseshoe cake created by Sylvia Weinstock.

## HOPPIN' NANCY

*Serves 6*

- 1 pound dried black-eyed peas
- 1 large onion, coarsely chopped
- 3 cloves garlic
- 2 bay leaves
- ¼ pound tasso ham, cubed
- ½ pound andouille sausage
- ½ cup chopped fresh parsley
- Salt and pepper to taste

**1.** Soak the beans overnight. Rinse and drain and pick through beans for debris.

**2.** In a large pot, add beans, onion, garlic, bay leaves and enough water to cover. Simmer for approximately two hours or until beans are tender. Drain.

**3.** Remove bay leaves. Add ham and sausage. Return beans to stove and cook for 10 minutes under medium heat. Add parsley and season with salt and pepper. Serve.

THE FOUR LEAVES OF CLOVER: ONE LEAF IS FOR HOPE, THE SECOND FOR FAITH, THE THIRD FOR LOVE, AND THE FOURTH FOR LUCK

# good luck gifts

I wouldn't say that I am irrationally superstitious...but you can never be too careful. To start the new year with positive karmic vigor, I decided to give each of my lunch guests a good luck amulet or care package. I bought a simple silver charm bracelet, attached two charms (a clover for luck and a heart for love) and had them engraved. I also made up baskets filled with tokens of luck and prosperity: a pink marzipan pig, sugared almonds, gold chocolate coins and a tin of open-pollinated Millennium seeds to symbolize a new beginning. I attached shipping tags to each gift and wrote a lucky quote on the back of each. Even a die-hard skeptic should be charmed...if I'm lucky.

Although the four leaves of the clover signify hope, faith, love and luck, it is the last two that I had engraved on the charm (*above*). If the Y2K doom and gloom predictions are true, my guests will have plenty of seeds to start on the road to self-sufficiency (*above right and opposite*). I found some helpful sites on the internet that allow you to search for an inspirational saying by keyword and copied them onto shipping labels (*right*).

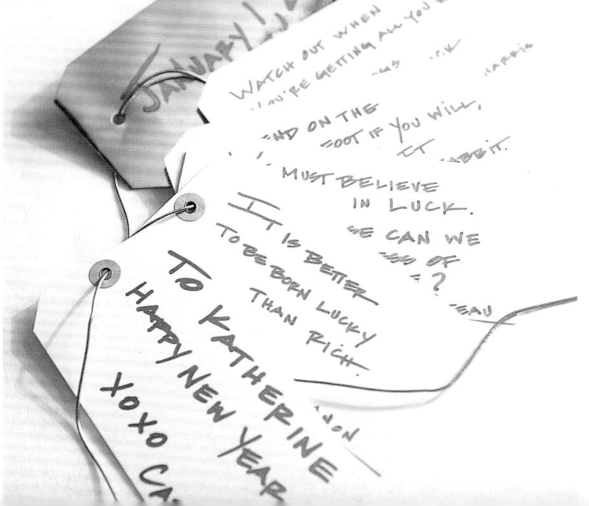

TO KATHERIN
HAPPY NEW YEA
XOXO
CAROLYN
Millennium
Victory Garden
who are concerned about being prepared we have
ther our best varieties for self-sufficiency and for
your own seed saving program into the future.
pollinated seed varieties for saving your own
CF325/S Cauliflower-Snow Peak
CN373/P Sweet Corn-Golden Bantam
CU402/P Cucumber-National Pickle
Kale-Winter Red

# GOOD LUCK QUOTES

I am a great believer in luck.
The harder I work the more of it I seem to have.
*~ Coleman Cox~*

What helps luck is a habit of watching for opportunities, of having a patient but restless mind, of sacrificing one's ease or vanity, or uniting a love of detail to foresight, and of passing through hard times bravely and cheerfully.
*~ Victor Cherbuliez ~*

It is better to be born lucky than rich.
*~Anonymous~*

Men of action are favored by the Goddess of luck.
*~ George S. Clason ~*

We must believe in luck. For how else can we explain the success of those we don't like?
*~ Jean Cocteau ~*

All of us have bad luck and good luck. The man who persists through the bad luck–who keeps right on going–is the man who is there when the good luck comes–and is ready to receive it.
*~ Robert Collier ~*

There is nothing we have to work so hard for as good luck.
*~Sarah Orne Jewett~*

A pound of pluck is worth a ton of luck.
*~ James A. Garfield ~*

Ten years from now I plan to be sitting here, looking out over my land. I hope I'll be writing books, but if not, I'll be on my pond fishing with my kids. I feel like the luckiest guy I know.
*~ John Grisham ~*

When I work fourteen hours a day, seven days a week, I get lucky.
*~ Dr. Armand Hammer ~*

Some folk want their luck buttered.
*~ Thomas Hardy ~*

The only sure thing about luck is that it will change.
*~ Bret Harte ~*

Luck is a dividend of sweat.
The more you sweat, the luckier you get.
*~ Ray Kroc ~*

Although men flatter themselves with their great actions, they are not so often the result of a great design as of chance.
*~ Francois De La Rochefoucauld ~*

Noticing a horseshoe hanging on the wall of Niels Bohr's (Nobel physicist) cottage, a visitor asked, "Can it be that you, of all people, believe it will bring you luck?" "Of course not," replied Bohr. "But I understand it brings you luck whether you believe it or not."

When God throws, the dice are loaded.
*~ Greek proverb ~*

Depend on the rabbit's foot if you will, but remember it didn't work for the rabbit.
*~ R. E. Shay ~*

I've found that luck is quite predictable.
If you want more luck, take more chances.
Be more active. Show up more often.
*~ Brian Tracy ~*

Success is just a matter of luck, all you need to do is ask a failure. History may be written by academics but it's rarely created by them.
*~ Source Unknown ~*

ADDITIONAL NOTES / INSPIRATIONS / REMEMBER NEXT YEAR

# FORCING BULBS & BRANCHES

I came late to the glory of forcing branches. About 10 years ago I was given the task of designing the flower arrangements for a charity benefit at the cavernous New York Public Library. I knew that a traditional bouquet of flowers would be dwarfed by the space, and I needed to make a big splash. Logistics prevented me from bringing in live trees, so I thought of the next best thing: tree limbs. The final gathering of 8-foot-tall crab apple branches was spectacular. The towering spires were in perfect proportion to the space. I learned from that experience that forced branches bring an architectural element into a room—they become sculpture. I translated the effect, scaled-down, for my home. Along with forced bulbs, branches are now a winter decorating staple, able to lift the gloom of dreary winter days. I began experimenting with pre-chilled bulbs my first Christmas at Weatherstone. I planted amaryllis, tulips, lily of the valley, paperwhites, ranunculus and hyacinth, trying my best to time the blooming to the holiday season. I was off by a few weeks. There were no blooms for the holidays and the ranunculus and lily of the valley barely made an appearance at all. Over the years I have refined the timing of the potting, and now produce enough flowers for holiday gifts and bouquets.

The snow was falling fast and furious outside and I thought it would be fun to try to recreate the same winter wonderland indoors. I set my luncheon table with clippings of white flowering cherry (*Prunus avium*) and tucked in sprigs of baby's breath (*Gypsophilia paniculata*) to hide the shins of the branches. As a reminder that spring would eventually arrive, I set pots of lily of the valley at two place settings. And to show that winter wasn't completely bereft of blossoms, I added two pots of the late-winter blooming *Helleborus niger*, or Christmas rose. I displayed the flowers in rustic wicker, which contrasted well with the purity of the white buds and table settings. In keeping with my snowfall theme, I used a dotted organdy tablecloth with matching napkins. Pure white china and small Saint-Cloud porcelain ginger jars marked each place. As you can see, one of the benefits of using branches for the center of the table is that they are so airy they don't obstruct your dinner companion's view.

*From left:* Small rustic wicker baskets hold individual arrangements of lily of the valley nestled with moss and ivy; baby's breath and Prunus echo the larger arrangement *(opposite)*; and *Helleborus niger*, the Christmas rose.

*personal notes:*

# branches

In general, branches from shrubs, such as the omnipresent forsythia, are easier to force than tree limbs. Both take about two weeks from the time of cutting, as long as their winter dormancy needs have been met: at least 8 weeks of temperatures below 40° F. (However, the closer the branches are cut to their actual time of blooming, the more readily they will blossom.) Cut branches a minimum of 6 inches long on a slant and bring indoors. Recut the stems and split the cut end about 2 inches with a knife to help speed water absorption. Place the recut branches in very hot water, about 125 to 150°, with a floral preservative and place in direct sunlight. Once the branches have bloomed, remove from direct light and keep cool (about 60° F) at night.

Some of the easier branches to force include magnolia (*opposite*), white and pink quince or Chaenomeles (*top and bottom left*), and flowering pink and white cherry or Prunus (*top and bottom right*). A full list of branches to force is included at the end of this chapter.

To keep branches fresh, recut about an inch off the bottom of the stems every couple of days and refill the container with clean warm water. Remove any buds or sideshoots that are under the water line.

# bulbs

By the end of February, I need strong reminders that spring is really on its way. Daffodils and tulips from the florist and forced bulbs from the greenhouse put me in a more optimistic frame of mind. In the arrangement above, I lined a wire basket and set floral foam inside as a base. The ring of parrot tulips, daffodils and *Lysimachia punctata* were pierced into the foam and two pots–hidden by the ring of flowers–of live mini-daffs were set on top of the foam. (I was so impressed by the vigorous Lysimachia as a cut flower that I plan to plant it in my perennial beds this spring, but I will have to keep an eye on it. Like most loosestrifes, Lysimachia is invasive.) I used the white Saint-Cloud jars as a decorative element and also as a pot for a miniature replica of the larger arrangement.

*Left:* Large pots of tulips are sometimes viewed best from above, when you can peer down into their faces.
*Below:* A sampling of forced corms and bulbs includes daffodils, hyacinth, amaryllis, ranunculus and paperwhites.
*Bottom:* Blue glass jars hold a collection of pink blooms from bulbs and branches.

# A MOSS GARDEN

Spring bulbs mounded with moss create a fairy playground. To assemble this live table-top garden, you can use a cookie sheet or a plastic sweater box lid for the base. I used a tray basket and lined it with a plastic garbage bag. I edged the tray with ivy and galax leaves and arranged live hyacinth, daffodils, lily of the valley, scilla, maidenhair fern and double campanula, all still in their plastic pots, inside the tray. I used ball moss and sheet moss to camouflage the ugly pots. Four blue-and-white china egg cups, each starring a different flower, were set at each place, and were highlighted by the Indian blue-and-white linens.

## TIP

*Mist the moss garden thoroughly once a day. Water potted plants with a long-nosed watering can. Remove to a cold room (about 50°) at night. Buy extra plants and ivy to replace fading blossoms.*

While I await the rebuilding of Weatherstone, I have moved into my four-room cottage, Weatherpebble. Three of the rooms are very small, but the living room (*above*), is vast and the ceilings are high. My apartment in Paris (*opposite*) is also quite small, but the ceilings are 14 feet high. I like to use branches in both these rooms because they seem to absorb the space, the arching sprays reaching up into the heights. I grouped the blue-and-white export china (*above*) saved from the fire in the middle of the room and filled it with all-white flowers: flowering cherry, stock, paperwhites, lily of the valley, camellias and white flowering quince. The bright white effect against the dark wood paneling was like snow falling on a forest floor. In Paris, I took the opposite tack: the colors melded rather than opposed. I borrowed the corals and pinks from the hand-painted taffeta curtains and paired the pink Prunus with tulips and camellia leaves.

## BRANCH FAVORITES

Branches for forcing can be found on a late winter walk, or they can be purchased from the florist or flower mart. These are the branches that I find the easiest to force:

*Cercis canadensis*
(Redbud)

Chaenomeles
(Japanese or Flowering Quince)

*Cornus florida*
(Flowering Dogwood)

*Hamamelis vernalis*
(Vernal Witch Hazel)

Crataegus
(Hawthorn)

Forsythisa

Lonicera
(Honeysuckle)

*Magnolia soulangiana*
(Saucer Magnolia)

*Magnolia stellata*
(Star Magnolia)

Malus
(Apple and Crabapple)

Prunus
(Flowering Almond, Cherry and Plum)

*Salix caprea*
(European Pussy Willow)

Spiraea
(Spirea)

Syringa
(Lilac)

Viburnum

ADDITIONAL NOTES / INSPIRATIONS / REMEMBER NEXT YEAR

# SOUPS

I would like to claim that I recall from my youth a cozy New England scene of fresh homemade soup simmering on the kitchen hearth accompanied by yeasty scents of freshly made bread. But I don't. I grew up in the Midwest with a can opener and a tin of Campbell's. I clearly remember a mug of Cream of Tomato soup and a grilled American cheese sandwich as the extent of my childhood lunchtime experience. But as an adult, I have made up for that fallow time and now pack my recipe repertoire with soups based on the best and freshest produce of the season. When the months turn cold, I turn to the root cellar and frozen garden produce. Winter squash, potatoes, dried beans, cabbage, onions and tomatoes (frozen whole from the summer glut) join chicken, veal, fish and beef stocks. Some years, if time allows, we get fussy about a proper stock, roasting cracked beef bones to add to a brunoise of leeks, carrots and celery, or simmering free-range chickens and straining the liquid into a clarified broth. But most often, I'll admit, I fall back on my childhood mastery of the can opener or a foil-wrapped cube to create my bouillon. Soup is a forgiving medium and it allows itself endless permutations. A little bit of this, a little leftover of that, cooked over gentle heat and you have a bowl of welcoming warmth to fight off the cold unkind winter.

*1.* Aigo Sau garnished with a rouille of garlic, red pepper, bread crumbs and olive oil. As an option, place a piece of toasted baguette rubbed with garlic on the bottom of the soup bowl and ladle soup on top.

## AIGO SAU (FISH SOUP)

*Serves 6*

- 2 pounds fresh cod or scrod
- 1 bulb fennel, coarsely chopped
- 3 stalks celery, coarsely chopped
- 5 to 6 medium potatoes, peeled and sliced ¼-inch thick
- 3 to 4 fresh plum tomatoes, chopped
- 1 leek, chopped
- 3 cloves garlic, finely chopped
- 1 medium onion, chopped
- 1 carrot, diced
- ¼ cup chopped parsley
- 2 bay leaves
- Juice and grated zest of 1 orange
- ⅓ cup olive oil
- ½ cup white wine
- Boiling water

1. In a 4-quart saucepan, layer all ingredients except the water in the order given. Add boiling water to cover.
2. Simmer for 20 minutes. Garnish with Rouille and serve.

### Rouille

*Makes ½ cup*

- 2 cloves garlic
- 1 tablespoon red pepper flakes
- 3 tablespoons plain bread crumbs
- 3 tablespoons olive oil
- ¼ cup broth from Aigo Sau

1. With a mortar and pestle or food processor, blend together the garlic, pepper flakes, bread crumbs and olive oil.
2. Add the fish stock and blend.

*2.* Cream of Chestnut Soup spiked with Sauternes.

## CREAM OF CHESTNUT SOUP

*Serves 6*

- 2 tablespoons butter
- ½ cup chopped shallots
- 1 cup Sauternes
- 4 cups chicken stock
- 1 15.5-ounce can purée of chestnuts
- ½ cup heavy cream
- 1 tablespoon balsamic vinegar
- ½ teaspoon salt
- ½ teaspoon pepper
- Chopped parsley for garnish

1. In a medium saucepan, heat butter on medium heat. Add shallots and sauté for 10 minutes,
2. Add Sauternes and cook an additional 10 minutes.
3. Add chicken stock, bring to a boil and reduce heat. Add chestnut purée and whisk until smooth.
4. Add cream, balsamic vinegar, salt, and pepper and simmer for 15 minutes. Serve immediately, garnished with chopped parsley.

Burro Val Casotto
Peso Netto g 250 e
con panna fresca
a mano nel calco di legno
1993
Château Bergeron
SAUTERNES
Appellation Sauternes Contrôlée
WHITE BORDEAUX WINE
MONSIEUR TOUTON SELECTION LTD NEW YORK - N.Y. U.S.A.
PRODUCT OF FRANCE
"Add water, broth or milk to obtain a desired consistency. Heat at low temperature.
Season to taste. Excellent with poultry, heat, venison"

2.

3.
WECK
Knorr

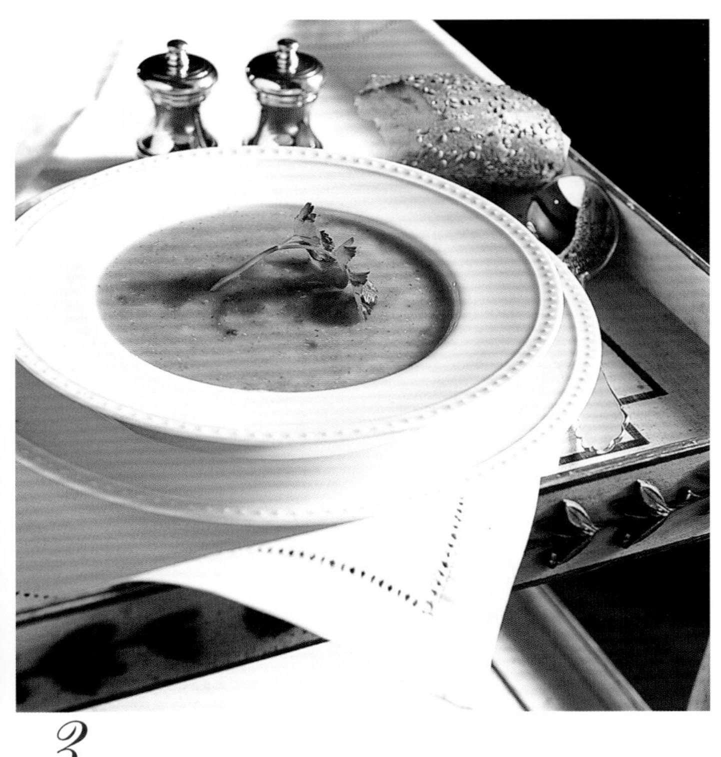

3. Garlic, Potato, and Parsley Soup salted with anchovies.

## GARLIC, POTATO & PARSLEY SOUP

*Serves 6 to 8*

3 tablespoons olive oil
1 head garlic, cloves peeled
4 anchovy filets
2 leeks, chopped
2 celery stalks, chopped
2½ pounds Yukon Gold potatoes, peeled and cut into 1-inch cubes
6 cups chicken stock
2 cups whole milk
Salt and freshly ground pepper
½ cup chopped parsley

1. Heat olive oil in a large saucepan over medium heat. Add garlic and anchovies and sauté for 4 to 5 minutes. Add leeks, celery and potatoes and sauté 10 more minutes.
2. Add chicken stock and potatoes and bring to boil. Reduce heat and simmer for 20 minutes or until potatoes are soft. Season with salt and pepper. Add parsley and milk, and remove from heat.
3. Cool soup slightly and working in small batches, purée in a food processor. Return soup to saucepan, reheat and serve immediately.

## MOROCCAN CHICKEN AND ROAST VEGETABLE SOUP

*Serves 6*

4 tablespoons olive oil
2 whole boneless chicken breasts
Salt and freshly ground pepper
2 cloves garlic, minced
2 cups diced onions
1 medium leek, diced
2-inch piece fresh ginger, minced
½ teaspoon ground cinnamon
1 small hot pepper, minced, or ½ teaspoon dried hot pepper flakes
1 teaspoon dried thyme
2 cups peeled, diced carrots
7 cups chicken stock
2 cups ½-inch peeled, diced sweet potatoes
1 cup ½-inch peeled, diced parsnips
1 cup ½-inch peeled, diced rutabagas
1 cup ½-inch peeled, diced turnips
1 15-ounce can chickpeas, drained and rinsed
1 14.5-ounce can whole tomatoes

1. Heat 2 tablespoons of oil in a large saucepan over medium heat. Season chicken breasts with salt and pepper and sauté until cooked through, about 8 minutes per side. Remove chicken from pan, allow to cool slightly, coarsely chop chicken into bite-size pieces and set aside.

*continued on page 107*

4. Moroccan Chicken and Roast Vegetable Soup relies heavily on the winter root cellar for its stock ingredients.

# 4.

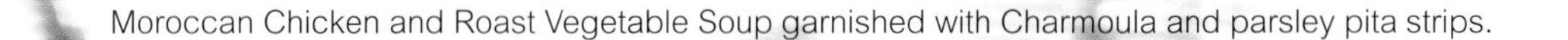

Moroccan Chicken and Roast Vegetable Soup garnished with Charmoula and parsley pita strips.

## winter spices

For a Moroccan, the presentation of a meal is ritualistic theater; sacrificing a lamb or chicken for your esteemed guest is the highest honor you can bestow. Although I didn't go farther than the freezer for my sacrifice, I did borrow from the scented spices of Morocco—ginger, cinnamon and thyme—to dress up my standard root cellar soup. If you can't flee to the Mediterranean during the bleak cold winter, you can at least cook as if you were there.

2. Heat remaining oil over medium heat in the saucepan and add garlic, onion, ginger and leeks. Sauté until tender, about 10 minutes.
3. Add cinnamon, hot pepper, thyme and carrots. Cook for 5 minutes on medium-high heat.
4. Add chicken stock, remaining root vegetables, chickpeas and tomatoes and bring to a boil. Reduce heat and simmer until the vegetables are tender, about 10 to 15 minutes.
5. Stir in reserved chicken pieces, salt and pepper, and simmer for another 5 minutes. Served topped with Charmoula.

### Charmoula

- ¼ cup raisins
- ¾ cup extra-virgin olive oil
- Zest and juice of 1 lemon
- 3 cloves garlic, minced
- 1 tablespoon paprika
- ¼ teaspoon ground cinnamon
- ½ inch piece of fresh ginger, minced
- 1½ teaspoons cumin
- ½ teaspoon honey
- ½ cup chopped parsley
- ½ cup chopped cilantro

1. Soak raisins in boiling water to cover for 10 minutes. Drain, rinse and allow to cool.
2. Mix raisins with remaining ingredients and stir well to combine.

## PASTA AND FENNEL SOUP

*Serves 6 to 8*

- 3 tablespoons olive oil
- 5 cloves garlic, chopped
- 1 cup finely chopped onions
- 1 large red pepper, seeded and finely chopped
- 2 cups finely chopped fennel (reserve fronds)
- 6 cups chicken broth
- 1½ cups tomato juice
- 1½ cups small uncooked pasta, such as ditalini or baby shells
- 1 teaspoon red pepper flakes, or to taste
- ½ teaspoon salt
- ¼ cup chopped fennel fronds

1. Heat olive oil in a large saucepan. Add garlic, onion, red pepper, and fennel and sauté over medium heat for 10 minutes, or until fennel is soft.
2. Add chicken broth and tomato juice. Simmer an additional 5 minutes then bring to a boil.
3. Add pasta, red pepper flakes and salt and boil until pasta is al dente, about 7 minutes. Add chopped fennel fronds and serve.

5. Pasta and Fennel Soup makes a satisfying meal in less than 30 minutes.

6.

# winter goodness

This simple herbal soup takes only minutes to prepare, and just as quickly brings to mind the aromatic flavors of Provençe. The woody astringent flavors of sage, thyme and bay leaf, coupled with the anise flavor of fennel, combine to make a tonic evocative of a warm Mediterranean breeze. Complete the illusion by serving the soup in a quimper faïance bowl with a poached egg atop a slice of rustic French bread.

*6.* Provençal Herb Soup topped with a poached egg and baguette toast.

## PROVENÇAL HERB SOUP

*Serves 6*

1 teaspoon olive oil
4 cloves garlic, minced
2 leeks, finely chopped
4 medium fresh tomatoes, seeded and chopped
1 small bulb fennel, chopped fine (reserve fronds)
6 cups boiling water
1 bay leaf
1 sprig fresh sage and thyme
Salt and freshly ground pepper
Juice and grated zest of 1 orange
Grated Parmesan cheese
6 eggs (optional)

1. Heat olive oil over medium heat in a large saucepan. Sauté garlic, leeks, tomatoes and fennel for about 10 minutes, or until tender.
2. Add boiling water to sautéed vegetables. Add bay leaf, sage, one fennel frond, and thyme to vegetables. Season with salt and pepper, add orange zest, and juice, and simmer another 10 minutes.
3. Remove the bay leaf and herb sprigs. At this point, you can poach eggs in the broth. Place a poached egg on a slice of toasted baguette and spoon the soup atop the toast. Sprinkle with cheese.

## FLAGEOLET BEAN SOUP

*Serves 6*

1 pound dried flageolet or small white beans, soaked overnight
1 small onion, quartered, plus 1 large onion coarsely chopped onion
2 bay leaves
3 stalks celery, chopped
4 cloves garlic, coarsely chopped
2 leeks, chopped
4 tablespoons olive oil
2 medium potatoes, peeled and diced into ½-inch cubes
4 carrots, peeled and diced into ½-inch cubes
1 tablespoon dried sage
2 ham hocks (optional)
1 14.5-ounce can whole tomatoes
¼ cup chopped parsley
1 pound charizo, sliced ⅛-inch thick
Salt and freshly ground pepper

1. Drain and rinse the soaked beans and combine with the quartered onion and bay leaves in a large saucepan. Bring to a boil, then reduce to a simmer. Cook for approximately 1½ hours, or until beans are tender, skimming the top as foam rises.
2. In a large saucepan over medium-high heat, sauté remaining chopped onion, garlic and leeks for 10 minutes.
3. Add carrots, potatoes, celery and sage and sauté for 5 minutes.

*7.* Flageolet Bean Soup gets its rustic flavors from charizo and ham hocks.

4. Remove the quartered onion and bay leaves from the beans and add beans and broth to the sautéed vegetables. (If adding ham hocks, the soup must be skimmed, and the ham hocks removed and meat added back to the pot before serving.) Add tomatoes and bring to a boil. Reduce heat and simmer for 15 minutes or until carrots and potatoes are tender.
5. Add parsley and chorizo, season with salt and pepper and cook 5 more minutes. Serve.

## LEMON ARTICHOKE SOUP

*Serves 6*

4 large fresh artichokes
Salt and freshly ground pepper
3 tablespoons olive oil
4 cloves garlic, coarsely chopped
1 cup chopped shallots
2 stalks celery, chopped
6 cups chicken stock
2 medium potatoes, peeled and cubed
¾ cup heavy cream
Juice of 1 lemon

1. Bring 2 quarts of salted water to a boil. Add artichokes and cook in boiling water for 35 to 45 minutes, or until leaves pull away easily. Remove the artichokes from the water and cool. Pull off all leaves and discard or reserve for another use. Remove inedible choke from the artichoke bottom and discard. Peel tough outer layer from stem, dice hearts and stems and set aside.
2. Heat olive oil in a large saucepan. Add garlic, shallots, celery and sauté for about 5 minutes or until shallots are translucent.

*continued on page 113*

7.

8.

8. Olive garnish makes a zesty finish for Lemon Artichoke Soup.

3. Add chicken stock and potatoes. Bring to a boil, reduce heat and simmer until the potatoes are done, about 10 to 15 minutes.
4. Add reserved diced artichokes and heavy cream. Cook for 5 minutes under medium heat. Remove from heat, allow to cool slightly, and working in small batches, purée in a blender or food processor.
5. Return purée to saucepan, stir in lemon juice, season with salt and pepper and reheat. Top each portion with 1 teaspoon olive garnish and serve.

## Olive Garnish

1 medium tomato, finely chopped
2 tablespoons chopped green olives
1 teaspoon grated lemon zest
1 teaspoon lemon juice
1 teaspoon chopped parsley

1. Combine all ingredients and stir until well blended.

# VALENTINE'S DAY

For years I celebrated Valentine's Day with a flamboyant display of my culinary skills, attempting to impress my beau of the moment. Inevitably, I got carried away. One year in particular, with all my fussing in the kitchen, dinner was still not ready an hour before midnight, when, after the obligatory bottle of champagne, the two of us were gaga from drink. As the candle wax melted and my feet ached from teetering on Manolo Blahnik heels all night, any pretentions to a romantic dinner for two died. My starving date had given up trying to keep me company in the kitchen and had settled in front of the television tuned to ESPN. With some tact, my friend said he was always pleased when someone cooked an elaborate meal for him, but all he really wanted was a cheeseburger. And I thought, you want it, you've got it, baby. No more overcooked pasta and sunken soufflés as I attempted to rekindle the fire, change the CD, or ooh and ahh over a love token. Even though I decided to take him at his word, that doesn't mean I couldn't stick to the theme of the heart. Armed with a set of cookie cutters, I created heart-shaped crudites, heart-shaped cheeseburgers, heart-shaped cottage fries, heart-shaped brownies with ice cream and hot fudge. Hardly a gourmet meal, but my date was charmed, and I was spared the exhaustion of trying to do a romantic multi-course dinner for two.

Floral foam is a life-saver when you need to make quick, theme-based arrangements for holidays or celebrations. The foam can be purchased from florists, craft stores and craft sections of superstores, in preshaped balls, bricks, topiary cones and hearts that adapt to countless creations; limited only by the sturdiness of the flowers' stems. Once it has been soaked, floral foam can easily be shaped with a sharp kitchen knife into any shape you choose, but keep in mind the foam can crumble if roughly treated. If you are going to hang your creation, consider that foam absorbs a large quantity of water and can be heavy. You can hang the foam with wire, hiding the wire behind a silk ribbon. For better stem stability on larger forms, wrap the foam with chicken wire before placing your flowers.

### HOW TO MAKE THE HEART WREATH *(page 114 and left)*

Follow the soaking direction on a 12-inch pre-formed floral-foam heart. Hang the heart in the sink and let the excess water drain out for about an hour. You will need (depending on how open the blooms are) about 2 bunches of red mini-carnations, 3 dozen magenta carnations and a dozen red ('Harvard') carnations. Cut all stems to $1\frac{1}{2}$ inches. Beginning on the inside of heart, push stems at an angle (stems pushed straight in may fall out) into the foam, clustering colors according to taste. Attach ribbon ends to form with thumbtacks, tie bow and hang.

### HOW TO MAKE THE HEART PLACE SETTING *(below and right)*

Soak floral foam according to package directions. Using a 4-inch heart-shaped cookie cutter, cut through an inch and a half of floral foam. Using a knife, bevel the edges of the heart. Cut the stems of a half a bunch of miniature carnations to one inch. Push stems into the heart foam at an angle. Display one heart on each place setting on a 9-inch plate.

Cookie-cutter foam hearts decorate each place setting.

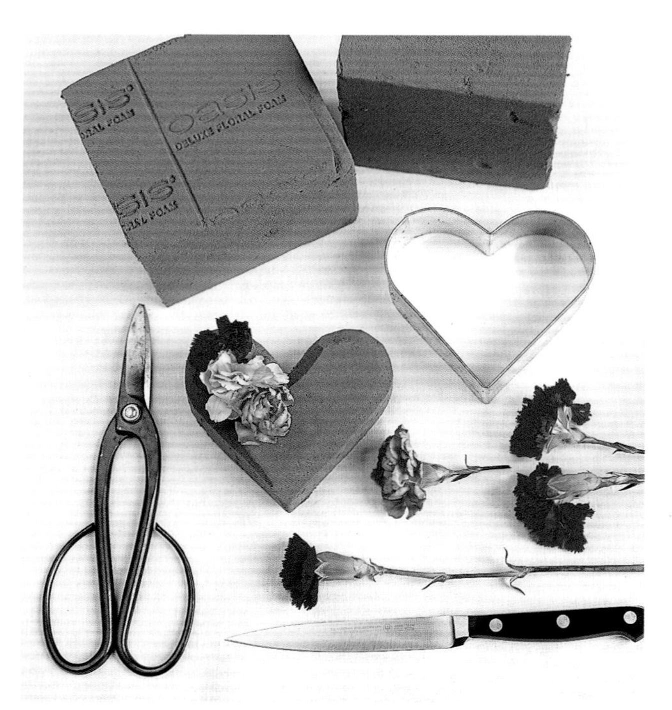

Katherine

*Below left:* I translated my beau's wish for just a cheeseburger, please, into a whimsical tea-time Valentine's Day table set with unadorned white porcelain and an informal bunch of deep-rose carnations tipped in white. I was so taken with the happy color combination of the lollipops that I searched for, and found, napkins to complement them. A 5-inch heart-shaped cookie cutter was used to cut the English muffin buns (*right*) and shape the burger patties (*below right*).

*Left and above right:* To put a little spin on the clichéd American meal of a hamburger and fries, I sliced large unpeeled baking potatoes 1/8-inch thick, and, with a 2-inch cookie cutter, formed the heart fries. I used the same size cookie cutter as I used to cut the hamburger to cut out the brownie (*opposite*) sprinkled with powdered sugar and topped with white violets. By using glass plates and plain white china, I kept the presentation very clean and simple.

A SIMPLE WHIMSICAL TEA
THAT COMES STRAIGHT FROM
THE HEART...

# TOPIARIES

In the fickle field of plant fashion, topiaries display remarkable staying power. I discovered potted herbaceous topiaries about two decades ago, but written evidence shows that the desire to sculpt trees, shrubs and plants began more than 2,000 years ago. Pliny the Elder credits Gnaius Mattius, a friend of Emperor Augustus, with adapting the pruning of plants from earlier Mediterranean and Asian cultures to shape the formal enclosed gardens of Roman aristocracy. By the seventeenth century elaborate topiary gardens had become the rage of the French and English courts, reaching their peak with the designs of André Le Nôtre, Louis XIV's landscape architect. Topiary gardens on such a grand scale requires constant clipping, pruning and training called for teams of landscapers, and years of patience. Today's topiary arts are more realistically accessible. Fast-growing herb topiaries, wire forms covered with vines and sphagnum moss balls supporting small-leafed creepers can be achieved in short order. In fact, one of my favorite topiaries (*see page 18*) is made with chicken-wire forms studded with boxwood clippings, and doesn't involve caring for live plants at all.

Topiary, the art of forming trees, shrubs, vines and plants into shapes, can be categorized into three groups: sphagnum moss topiaries, wire form topiaries and standard topiaries. Garden topiaries, such as boxwood or yew mazes and germander knot gardens are summertime activities and will not be dealt with here.

Sphagnum moss topiaries are wire forms stuffed with moss (available ready-made at garden centers and florists). The forms come in various geometric or animal shapes. Small-leaf vines or creepers are planted in the moss and florists' staples are used to attach the leaders around the form. This is the quickest and easiest topiary method; little or no pruning is necessary.

Wire form topiaries, usually hoops, balls, hearts and cones, provide a support for small-leafed or medium-leafed vines to train on. As the vine grows the leaders are tucked into and around the frame. Once the frame is filled in with growth, minimum pruning is needed to keep the form defined.

Trees, shrubs and plants trained to grow vertically with a central leader are called standard topiaries. By gradually pruning the lower branches of a staked young tree or shrub, a central trunk will form followed by foliage above, which is pruned into a globe. Softwood standard trunks can also be manipulated to grow in spirals or braids. Since it is essential that the training and pruning be done gradually, standards are the most labor-intensive and time-consuming of the three types of topiary.

*personal notes:*

On a recent trip to Paris, I found that Louis XIV's topiary arts live on (*right*). After my house burned, I recreated my own romantic Louis XIV corner at Weatherpebble, with a canopied bed flanked with white azalea standards (*above*).

## TIP

*For proper balance and to give the standard enough green to photosynthesize, the lollipop head of a standard should measure one-third of the total length of the stem.*

At my goddaughter's christening in Paris, the organdy-topped tables were decorated with wire topiary hearts supporting tiny runners of *Soleirolia soleirolii*, more commonly known as baby's tears or–more hopefully fitting–peace-in-the-home. The hand-painted organdy curtain with my goddaughter's initials filtered the sun, creating a soothing, gentle light in the room.

TOPIARY HEARTS COVERED WITH BABY'S TEARS REPRESENT THE LOVE FOR MY GODDAUGHTER ON HER CHRISTENING DAY

# fruits & flowers

I found this heart-shaped topiary trained with *Hedera colchica* (Persian ivy) at a market in Paris and made it the centerpiece of an informal luncheon, but it would be just as suitable for a Valentine's Day or wedding anniversary decoration. So that the heart wouldn't be lonely, I added four small azalea topiaries. To unify the plants, I potted them in similar straw baskets, and blanketed each with moss. The fragile stems of the azaleas were supported with bamboo sticks and tied to the bamboo with chartreuse raffia, a color picked up from the antique quilt I used as a tablecloth.

During the winter, while the lucky ones are away and lying on the beach, I escape into my small greenhouse when I need a shot of warmth and vitamin D. I have a pair of large bay topiaries and citrus trees that I've lovingly tended for years, and they haven't quit on me yet. I have given small lunches and dinners in this unexpected climate, and guests seem to enjoy it more than a roaring fire. They are delighted by the warmth and the exotic scent of jasmine and gardenia. Potted primroses hold the place cards and topiaries of myrtle surround a calamondin (an excellent indoor citrus) and bowls of grocery-store kumquats.

I planted three large straw baskets with fraises des bois (alpine strawberries) and trained the runners around simple wire hoops. Topiary baskets are lined with plastic pots (so soil and water don't leak out). The soil at the tops of the baskets is covered with moss. Three smaller baskets were filled with the tiny fresh strawberries and once the brunch was over, we ate the table decorations for dessert.

*personal notes:*

Those who don't have the time or patience to train unruly vines or shrubs can achieve the same geometric effect with sprigs of boxwood or other small-leafed woody greens, a block of floral foam, and an attractive container. I often use these inexpensive (less than twenty dollars) silver-plated beakers or julep cups from India as a base, fill them with soaked foam, and clip the boxwood into globes. These topiaries are simple to make and can last for days. Also, as we discovered, they can be frozen if given a good misting before hand, and used or reused at a later date.

## HOW TO MAKE A BOXWOOD TOPIARY

***Materials Needed:***

1 case (or less depending on size of container) of florist boxwood
1 large block floral foam
Vase, bowl or terra cotta pot with liner
Knife
Scissors

1. Float foam in water for a minute or two or until the foam is completely saturated. Drain and place on a waterproof surface or in a large plastic box to catch water.
2. With a sharp kitchen knife, cut the foam to the approximate shape of your container to about an inch below the rim. Refine the shape by whittling pieces off the foam until it fits snugly in the container.
3. Starting at the top, push pieces of boxwood (select the new growth tips) into the foam, approximating the final shape you wish to achieve.
4. Trim the boxwood with scissors into the final shape. If you are making a large topiary, use round wire hoops (for globes) as a guide when cutting, or if you are making a cone, tie two bamboo poles together at one end to form a vee. Set the vee over the boxwood, adjusting the angle as necessary, and follow the lines of the bamboo "vee" as you trim.

# PLANTS TO TRAIN

## PLANTS TO TRAIN ON SPHAGNUM MOSS TOPIARIES

*Ficus pumila* 'Minima' (Creeping Fig)

*Ipomoea acuminata* (Morning Glory)

*Laurentia fluviatilis* (Blue Star Creeper)

*Lindneria grandiflora* (Angel's Tears)

*Saxifragia stolonifera* (Strawberry Begonia)

*Soleirolia* (Baby's Tears)

*Viola hederacea* (Tasmanian Violet)

## PLANTS TO TRAIN ON WIRE FORMS

*Cissus striata* (Miniature Grape Ivy)

*Cymbalaria muralis* (Kenilworth Ivy)

*Hedera helix* (various small-leafed ivies)

*Hoya carnosa* (Wax Plant)

*Jasminum polyanthum* (Winter Jasmine)

*Philodendron scandens* (Money Plant)

*Rhoicissus rhomboidea* (Grape Ivy)

*Solanum jasminoides* (Potato Vine)

*Trachelospermum asiaticum*

## PLANTS TO TRAIN AS TOPIARY STANDARDS

*Abutilon pictum* 'Thompsoni' (Flowering Maple)

*Anisodontea hypomandarum* (African Mallow)

Bougainvillea

Fuchsia

*Genista canariensis* (Canary Island Broom)

*Lantana camara* (Common Lantana)

*Laurus nobilis* (Sweet Bay)

Lavender

*Myrtus communis* 'Microphylla' (Myrtle)

*Pelargonium concolor* (Scented Geranium)

Rosemary

ADDITIONAL NOTES / INSPIRATIONS / REMEMBER NEXT YEAR

# ENDPAPERS

## THE GARDEN IN WINTER

*"As I write, snow is falling outside my Maine window, and indoors all around me half a hundred garden catalogues are in bloom." —Katherine S. White*

Gardening catalogues begin arriving soon after Thanksgiving, just in time to give the die-hard gardener a ray of hope. Winter months can be spent poring over the wish books, drawing up lists of coveted seeds and plants. But winter isn't all about dreamy plant lust, there are also chores to be done. Spring is crunch time for gardeners, so it pays to be prepared. Use this dead time to get yourself in gear for the upcoming thaw:

### WINTER CHECKLIST

- *Draw and finalize perennial and vegetable garden plans. Use a software program if you are fluent in CAD. If not, it's a good time to learn computer landscaping.*
- *Make a list of plants to move (you marked them with red ribbon in late summer, remember?) to a more suitable location in the spring.*
- *Check germination of seeds by pre-sprouting in damp paper towels. (Most seeds except onions, lettuce, carrots and delphinium are viable for a few years if stored properly in plastic boxes with a desiccant such as silica gel.)*
- *Make a list of fresh seed needed. Don't forget potatoes and summer bulbs.*

*From top:* Boxwood is not reliably hardy in the northwest corner of Connecticut, so we guard the shrubs with burlap fences. Nora keeps meticulous records of all seeds ordered, dates sown and germination dates. Cool-loving seedlings such as lettuce and spinach begin their life in the hoop houses and will be planted in the potager in spring.

- *Happily devour seed and plant catalogues. List your desires on Post-It notes and affix to the front of each catalogue. Review the lists, then get realistic, and prune them down to an affordable size.*

- *Phone, fax, mail or order seeds and plants online as early as possible because featured selections run out quickly. Keep a list of items ordered.*

- *Organize a seed swap with friends and trade last year's leftover seeds. Provide small envelopes and a decorative rubber stamp for labeling.*

- *Schedule seed sowing times (peppers and eggplant are usually first), counting back from the last frost date expected. Mark dates on a gardening calendar and display it in plain view.*

- *Order seed sowing supplies: Seed-starting mix, peat pots, wooden labels, permanent marker, seedling fertilizer, heatmats and plastic flats. Check grow lights and replace if weakening.*

- *Check stored bulbs and tubers for rot. Compost sprouting onions, but not diseased bulbs and tubers.*

- *During thaws, inspect perennials for heaving. Mulch heaved plants; do not push them back into the soil by dancing around the crowns. In spring, dig up heaved plants and replant.*

- *Scatter fireplace ashes–sparingly–in beds or areas that need a higher soil pH.*

- *Get lawnmower and rototiller tuned up, spark plugs replaced and oil filters cleaned.*

- *Risk a small mid-March planting of peas, mâche and spinach.*

# IN MEMORY OF STONELEIGH

Stoneleigh, my eccentric Scottish terrier, died on Christmas Eve. I now find myself going to the places she loved to sit—on a certain pillow, a piece of furniture or at the edge of the bridge where she would sit for hours gazing at the frogs in the Weatherstone ponds. We laughingly called her Miss Froggy as she would peer into the murky pond for hours trying to snare her antagonist, the Frog. Stoneleigh was a free-spirited loner, but she still needed affection from me. She was the ever-patient friend and teacher to Annie, the Cairn youngster. It is strange and sad that now Annie sits at Stone's place at the pond waiting for the Frog, and lies on Stone's pillow. Annie misses her friend and companion. I see Annie staring sadly, or trotting solo around the property and I feel she is always looking for Stoneleigh. As I am.

# CONTRIBUTORS

**Melissa Davis** has discovered that there are 22 possible synonyms for the word "grow," and even that isn't enough.

**Sylvie Becquet** captures the beauty of all that is Weatherstone while toting a camera bag that weighs more than she does.

**Alan Richardson** kindly puts his decade-long obsession with Tuscany on hold while he and Alessandra focus their collective eye on Weatherstone.

Armed with a case of floral foam and a can of spray paint, **Susan Poglitsch** conquers the holiday season with unflagging zeal.

**Nancy Quattrini** spent the winter stirring the Weatherstone soup cauldron and inventing new ways to elevate the humble spud.

**Placido** and **Margarida de Carvalho** double-team as the captains of Weatherstone, a ship that, thanks to them, runs smoothly despite the snowstorm.

In winter **Nora Holmes** doesn't go dormant with the plants. She can be found in the basement of the greenhouse perfecting the science of forcing bulbs.

If there is a marzipan pig or a pinecone candle to be found in New York City, **Molly McCarthy** will track it down pronto.

**Rosa Costa** has earned many friends and followers from her enthusiastic and helpful advice on the 800 line. She can also turn out a stunning paella blindfolded.

**Joel Minton** and **Randy Krakenberg** plow ahead all winter long. They have recently been sighted looking wistfully at the lawn tractor.

The old guard dogs **Pookie** and **Annie** have been joined by two tyros: **Ruffy**, a Wheaten terrier, and **Winnie**, a Cairn. Pookie and Annie have introduced the newcomers to the delights of snow-sniffing and, come spring, will teach them how to dig up newly planted perennials.

To the Sharon, Lakeville, West Cornwall, Falls Village, Amenia, Wassaic and Dover Plains volunteer fire departments: I will never be able to thank you enough.

# SOURCE GUIDE

### HELLEBORES

www.gardenweb.com/cyberplt/plants/hellebor.html
www.btinternet.com/~farmyard.nurseries

Jim and Jenny Archibald
'Bryn Collen'
Ffostrasol, Llandysul
Dyfed, Wales SA44 5SB
Seed suppliers (seeds can be imported into United States).

Carroll Gardens
444 East Main Street
Westminster, MD 21157
Tel: 410-848-5422
Fax: 410-857-4112

Heronswood Nursery
7530 NE 288th Street
Kingston, WA 98346
Tel: 360-297-4172
Fax: 360-297-8321
www.heronswood.com

Thompson & Morgan
P.O. Box 1308
Jackson, NJ 08527
Tel: 800-274-7333
Fax: 888-466-4769
www.thompson-morgan.com
Hybrid and species hellebore seed.

### HOLIDAY PLANNING

L'Occitane
Tel: 888-623-2880
Provençal scented linen water.

### A CHRISTMAS PARTY

Central Shippee
P.O. Box 13546
Star Lake Rd.
Bloomingdale, NJ 07403
Tel: 973-838-1100
www.centralshippee.com
Felt and felt materials.

Crate & Barrel
650 Madison Ave.
New York, NY 10022
Tel: 212-308-0011
www.crateandbarrel.com
Large red mercury balls and red wine glasses.

Singing group at party:
Carl Phipps, Bethel Gospel Assembly
E-mail: CTP1520@aol.com
Tel: 212-860-1520

### POTATOES

Irish Eyes with a Hint of Garlic
(Formerly Ronniger's Seed & Potato Co.)
P.O. Box 307
Ellensburg, WA 98926
Tel: 509-925-6025
Fax: 800-964-9210
www.irish-eyes.com
An huge collection of potato seed (online catalogue) from fingerlings to Russets.

### CARNATIONS

Rand B. Lee
President
The American Dianthus Society
PO Box 22232
Santa Fe, NM 87502-2232
Tel: 505-438-7038

### MILLENNIUM LUNCH

Elk Candy Co.
1628 Second Ave.
New York, NY 10028
Tel: 212-585-2303
www.citysearch.com/nyc/elkcandy
Marzipan pigs.

Territorial Seed Company
P.O. Box 157
Cottage Grove, OR 97424
Tel: 541-942-9547
Open-pollinated seeds packaged for a millennium garden.

Tiffany's
727 Fifth Ave.
New York, NY 10022
Tel: 212-755-8000
www.tiffany.com
Bracelet, charms and engraving.

### FORCING BULBS AND BRANCHES

U.S. Evergreen
805 6th Ave.
New York, NY 10001
Tel: 212-741-5300

### VALENTINE'S DAY

Anderson Floral Supply Inc.
P.O. Box 526
Celeron, NY 14720
Tel: 716-665-5197
www.afloral.com/index.html

Culinary Store
www.culinarystore.com
Set of 5-, 3- and 2-inch heart-shaped copper cookie cutters available to order on line.

Williams Sonoma
1-800-541-2233
Lollipops.

### TOPIARIES

For topiary supplies:
www.topiaryart.com
www.topiaryinc.com
For a virtual tour of famed topiary gardens (click on "Tours").

Logee's Greenhouses, Ltd.
141 North Street
Danielson, CT 06239-1939
Tel: 888-330-8038
Tender topiary plants.

Two's Company
30 Warren Place
Mt. Vernon, NY 10550
Tel: 800-896-7266
Silver-plated beaker or julip cup.

### ENDPAPERS

The online ZDNet Software Library offers a wide variety of shareware and freeware programs of interest to gardeners including gardening journals, garden design, seed databases, seed-starting calendars, and plant propagation. To access, type "ZDNet Software Library" into your browser's search engine.

### PHOTOGRAPHY

***Sylvie Becquet***
Cover, intro, 1-13, 16, 18, 20-26, 30, 32, 34-39, 41, 47, 54-67, 72-74, 84-95, 97, 114-126, 128-129, 131, 135-136

***Alan Richardson***
16, 18, 27, 31-33, 40-41, 44-45, 47-52, 76-81, 85, 96, 100-113, 121, 123, 127, 130, 134

***Melanie Acevedo***
68-71, 74-75

***Carolyne Roehm***
137